Mrs Beeton's
Favorite Sweet Dishes

Caramel Rice Pudding

Mrs Beeton's Favorite Sweet Dishes

Edited by
Maggie Black

THE BOBBS-MERRILL COMPANY, INC.
Indianapolis • New York

We wish to thank Richard A. Ahrens and Arlene S. Bickel for their
assistance in putting this book together.

Contents

Weights and Measures Used in This Book

60 drops	1 teaspoon	Liquid measures
3 teaspoons	1 tablespoon	
4 tablespoons	¼ cup	
1 cup	½ pint	
2 cups	1 pint	
2 pints	1 quart	
4 quarts	1 gallon	

Solid measures

Spoons are standard teaspoons and tablespoons, which hold the amounts of liquid given above. They are measured with the contents leveled off, i.e. all the spoonfuls are level spoonfuls.

The cup is a standard measuring cup that holds 8 fluid oz. or ½ pint.

Solid measures

Flour, sifted	4 tablespoons	1 oz.
Granulated sugar	2 tablespoons	1 oz.
Confectioners' sugar, sifted	4 tablespoons	1 oz.
Butter or margarine	2 tablespoons	1 oz.
Cornstarch	4 tablespoons	1 oz.
Granulated or powdered gelatin	3 tablespoons	1 oz.
Corn syrup or molasses	1 tablespoon	1 oz.
Flour, sifted	1 cup	4 oz.
Granulated sugar	1 cup	8 oz.
Confectioners' sugar, sifted	1 cup	4 oz.
Butter or margarine	1 cup	8 oz.
Cornstarch	1 cup	4 oz.
Corn syrup or molasses	1 cup	1 lb.

Metric measures

Precise metric equivalents are not very useful. The weights are almost impossible to measure accurately and are not used in ordinary cooking.

Schools use a 25-gram unit for 1 oz. and for retested recipes. This means that they can use existing equipment. For instance, a 6-inch sandwich tin can be used for a 15-cm. one, and a 7-inch tin for an 18-cm. one. Yorkshire pudding using 100 grams plain flour fits into a 2×14 cm. ($8 \times 5\frac{1}{2}$ in.) baking pan.

Mrs. Beeton's recipes are all being retested so that they can be converted to metric measures when these come into general use.

Oven temperatures

	Fahrenheit	Celsius
Very cool	225 °F	110 °C
Very cool	250 °F	130 °C
Very cool	275 °F	140 °C
Cool	300 °F	150 °C
Warm	325 °F	170 °C
Moderate	350 °F	180 °C
Fairly hot	375 °F	190 °C
Fairly hot	400 °F	200 °C
Hot	425 °F	220 °C
Very hot	450 °F	230 °C
Very hot	475 °F	240 °C

Deep fat frying table

Food	Bread Browns in	Fat Temp	Oil Temp
Uncooked mixtures, e.g. fritters	1 minute	370-375 °F	375-385 °F
Cooked mixtures, e.g. fish cakes	40 seconds	380-385 °F	385 °F
Fish	1 minute	375 °F	375 °F
Potato straws, French fries, chips, etc.	20 seconds	390 °F	395 °F

Introduction

Here is a selection of various kinds of sweet dishes that people around the globe have come to like and use. They include hot and cold milk puddings; custards; batter dishes, in both pancake and fritter styles; soufflés and omelets; pies; flans and tarts; and steamed, boiled, and baked hot puddings. There are molded desserts such as jellies, creams, trifles, fruit purees and fools, and meringue dishes. Finally, there are sections on gâteaux, various icings and fillings, petits fours and sweetmeats, and on preserves for the cupboard in which anyone can take pride.

Some of these sweet dishes are simple. Others are rich, luscious confections. All are "classics," whether made by traditional means, or using the new products that modern technology provides. They should all have a place in any civilized cookery repertoire.

Hot Milk Puddings and Custards

These milk-based puddings may be plain and light or luxuriously rich. This depends on whether they contain cream or a lot of eggs or expensive ingredients such as ground almonds or liqueurs.

They can all be simmered or "boiled," or baked; or they can be steamed and unmolded like a jelly, if they contain enough eggs. They must always be cooked very gently and slowly. They are usually flavored by soaking a plant flavoring in the warmed milk (e.g. bay leaf or lemon rind), with a powdered herb or spice such as ground cinnamon, or with a liquid such as vanilla extract or a liqueur. There is almost no end to the variations you can make by using the basic recipes here.

TRADITIONAL RICE PUDDING (and All Other Large-Grain Milk Puddings, using Sago, Tapioca, etc.)

²/₃ cup grain, any type	1 tbs. finely shredded suet *or* butter
5 cups milk	
¼-³/₈ cup sugar	Grated nutmeg *or* similar flavoring

Grease a baking dish. Wash the grain in cold water, if necessary, and put it into the dish with the milk. Let stand for ½ hr. Add the sugar, flake on the fat, if used, and sprinkle on the flavoring. Bake very slowly (150 °C, 310 °F) until the pudding is thick and creamy and is brown on top — a minimum of 2-2½ hr. (The pudding is better if it cooks even more slowly for 4-5 hr.)

Note: If a flavoring extract is used, it is mixed into the milk before cooking. If dried or canned milk is used, reduce the amount of rice to ½ cup, use the amount of milk product that makes up to 1 qt., and cook at 140 °C, 275 °F, for at least 3½-4 hr.

For puddings with eggs, use:

²/₃ cup large grain, any type	2-4 eggs
5 cups milk	¼-³/₈ cup sugar
	Flavoring

Wash the grain in cold water, if necessary. Put the grain and milk into a strong or double saucepan, and cook slowly until the grain is tender. Remove from the heat and allow to cool slightly. Separate the eggs and beat the whites until stiff. Stir into the pudding the slightly beaten egg yolks, sugar and flavorings, and, lastly,

2

fold in the beaten whites. Pour into a well-buttered baking dish and bake in a warm oven (170 °C, 335 °F) for about 40 min., until the top is brown.

4-6 servings

CARAMEL-RICE PUDDING

³⁄₈ cup sugar	2 eggs
5 tbs. water	3 tbs. sugar
³⁄₄ cup rice	Pinch of salt
1 qt. milk	

Heat a charlotte mold and have ready a thickly folded band of newspaper so that the hot mold can be circled with it and held firmly in one hand. Prepare the caramel by heating the ³⁄₈ cup sugar and water together; stir until it boils; then remove the spoon and allow to boil, without stirring, until golden brown. Immediately pour the caramel into the warmed charlotte mold and twist it around until the sides and base are well-coated.

Wash the rice and simmer it in the milk with the salt until it is soft and all the milk has been absorbed. Cool slightly, and stir in the beaten eggs and sugar. Turn into the caramel-lined mold, cover closely with greased paper, and steam for 1 hr., until firm. Serve either hot or cold.

6 servings

MEDIUM- AND SMALL-GRAIN MILK PUDDINGS
(Semolina, ground rice, small sago, crushed tapioca)

5 cups milk	³⁄₄ cup grain, any
Flavoring	type above
	¹⁄₄-³⁄₈ cup sugar

Heat the milk and infuse a stick or peel flavoring, if used, for about 10 min. Remove the flavoring. Sprinkle the grain into the milk, stirring quickly to prevent lumps. Place over heat and continue stirring while the milk simmers, until the grain is transparent and cooked through; this takes about 15 min. Add the sugar and any flavoring extract used. The pudding can then be served as it is, hot or cold, or can be poured into a well-buttered baking dish and baked in a moderate oven (180 °C, 350 °F) for 20-30 min., until the top has browned.

For puddings with eggs, use:

5 cups milk	2-4 eggs
Flavoring	¹⁄₄-³⁄₈ cup sugar
³⁄₄ cup grain, any type in previous recipe	

Heat the milk and infuse any stick flavoring used for about 10 min. Then remove it. Sprinkle the grain into the flavored milk, stirring quickly to prevent lumps. Continue stirring for about 15 min., until the grain has become transparent and cooked through. Allow to cool slightly. Stir in the slightly beaten egg yolks. Add the sugar and flavoring extract, if used, and, lastly, fold in the egg whites, whisked until stiff. Pour the mixture into a well-buttered pie or casserole dish and bake in a warm oven (170 °C, 335 °F) until the top is brown. This takes 30-40 min.

6 servings

POWDERED-GRAIN PUDDINGS
(Arrowroot, cornstarch, custard powder, finely ground rice, powdered barley, fine oatmeal)

⁵⁄₈ cup grain, any type above	¹⁄₄-³⁄₈ cup sugar
5 cups milk	Flavoring

Mix the grain to a paste with a little of the milk and put the rest of the milk on to boil. Pour the boiling milk onto the blended paste, stirring briskly to prevent lumps. Return the mixture to the saucepan, heat until it thickens, then simmer for 2-3 min., to cook the grain. Add the sugar. The pudding can then be served, or poured into a baking dish and baked for 20-30 min. at 180 °C, 350 °F until the top is browned.

For puddings with eggs, use:

⁵⁄₈ cup powdered grain, any type	2-4 eggs
	¹⁄₄-³⁄₈ cup sugar
5 cups milk	Flavoring

Cook the grain completely as in the previous recipe. Let the mixture cool.

Separate the eggs and beat the whites until stiff. Beat the yolks slightly and stir them into the pudding with the sugar and any flavoring extract used. Lastly, fold in the beaten whites. Pour the mixture into a well-buttered baking dish, and bake in a warm oven (170 °C, 335 °F) for about 30 min., until the top has browned. Sprinkle with brown sugar and/or butter flakes before baking, if you wish.

6 servings

TIMBALE OF SEMOLINA

2½ cups milk	6-7 apricot halves
¾ cup semolina	⅝ cup apricot
¼ cup sugar	syrup
2 tbs. cream	Maraschino
	liquid (optional)

Timbale of Semolina

Decoration:

Glacé cherries	Angelica
Almonds	

Heat the milk, sprinkle in the semolina, stirring briskly, and simmer until it is cooked through. Cool slightly; then add the sugar and vanilla extract. Separate the eggs and stir the beaten yolks into the milk mixture. Beat until the mixture is nearly cold. Add the cream and lightly fold in the stiffly beaten egg whites. Three-quarters fill a well-greased timbale or 6 small dariole molds with the mixture. Cover with greased paper. Steam small molds for about ½ hr., until set — a large mold for about ¾ hr.

Meanwhile, the heat the apricots. Boil the apricot syrup until well-reduced, and flavor with a little maraschino liqueur if you wish.

Traditional Rice Pudding

When the pudding is cooked and set, un-mold onto a hot dish. Place ½ an apricot on top of each small mold and decorate with a glacé cherry, chopped almonds, and angelica. Treat a large mold similarly. Pour the syrup around, and serve.

RICE CROQUETTES

⅔ cup rice	¼ cup sugar
1 qt. milk	1 egg
Pinch of salt	Egg and white
1 tbs. butter	bread
Lemon rind	crumbs
	Frying fat

Wash and drain the rice; put it into a pan with the milk, salt, butter, and thinly cut lemon rind. Cook until the rice is tender, all the milk absorbed, and the mixture is thick. Remove the lemon rind. Add the sugar and beaten egg, and reheat to cook the egg. Spread the mixture on a plate and let cool. When almost cold, form into pear or cork shapes and coat with egg and crumbs. Fry in deep fat that is just begin-ning to haze. Cook until golden brown. Drain well. Dredge well with sugar, and serve.

Note: If shallow fat is used, it should come halfway up the croquette and then the croquette must be turned over.

6 servings

CUSTARDS, VARIOUS — TO COOK

Pouring Custards These are made by heat-ing the mixture and keeping it at a temper-ature *below* boiling point until the eggs are cooked evenly throughout. Doing this in a double boiler lessens the risk of curdling.

5

Baked Custards The dish to contain the custard should be well-greased. When filled, it should be placed in a tray of warm water. Bake slowly at about 170 °C, 325 °F until the custard is set. Take it out of the water at once to prevent further cooking.

Steamed Custards The bowl must be well-greased, and the custard covered with greased paper to prevent dripping condensed steam falling into it. Only a very gentle flow of steam should be allowed.

A custard that is going to be unmolded needs at least 4 eggs to 2½ cups liquid or it will break when being turned out.

BAKED OR STEAMED CUSTARD

1 qt. milk	3-4 eggs for a
Flavoring	baked custard,
Wine Sauce	plus 1 more for a
2-3 tbs. sugar	steamed custard

Beat the eggs with the sugar. Warm the milk and flavoring and add gradually to the egg mixture, stirring well. Pour the mixture into a greased pie or casserole dish for a baked custard or into a buttered mold for a steamed one. Stand the dish in a tray of warm water and bake in a warm oven (170 °C, 325-335 °F) for about 50 min. For a steamed custard, cover the mold with greased paper, secure it firmly, and steam gently for about 40 min., until the custard is set in the center. Turn out and serve with Wine Sauce.

5-6 servings

BREAD-AND-BUTTER PUDDING

6 thin slices of	3 eggs
bread and butter	3 tbs. sugar
⅜ cup currants	1 qt. milk
or stoned	
raisins or chopped	
candied peel	

Grease a 5 cup baking dish. Remove the bread crusts if you wish. Then cut the bread into squares or triangles and lay them neatly in the dish. Sprinkle fruit over each layer. Beat the eggs with the sugar, add the milk, and pour the mixture over

the bread. It should only half-fill the dish. Allow to soak for at least 30 min. Then bake for about 1 hr. in a moderate oven (180 °C, 350 °F), until the custard is set.

5 – 6 servings

CABINET PUDDING

1 medium	2½ cups milk
sponge cake or	4 eggs
12 ladyfingers	A few drops of
8 ratafia biscuits	vanilla extract
2 tbs. sugar	

Decoration:

Angelica	Glacé cherries

Grease a 2½ cup soufflé (straight-sided) mold, and put a round of greased paper in the bottom, to fit exactly. Decorate the bottom of the mold with a bold design of cherries and angelica. Line the sides with slices of cut sponge cakes or ladyfingers. Crumble the trimmings of cake and ratafias and put them into the mold.

Add the sugar to the milk, and warm slightly. Add the well-beaten eggs and vanilla extract. Pour the mixture into mold and let stand for about 1 hr., if time allows. Cover with greased paper and steam gently 1-1¼ hr. Remove paper, turn out, and peel off top paper. Serve with Jam Sauce.

6 servings   Cooking time – 1-1¼ hr.

CARAMEL CUSTARD

⅜ cup sugar	1 pt. milk
5 tbs. cold water	A few drops of
4 eggs	vanilla extract
2 tbs. sugar	

Have ready a warm charlotte or plain mold. Prepare caramel with sugar and water, and line the mold as for Caramel Rice Pudding above.

Work together the eggs and sugar without beating them, and pour the warmed milk over them. Add the vanilla extract. Strain the custard into the mold, and cover with greased paper. Steam very slowly for about ¾ hr., until the custard is set in the center; or stand the custard uncovered in a tray of warm water and bake in a warm oven (170°C, 335 °F) until the center is set. This takes about 40 min. Turn the custard out carefully so that the caramel runs off and serves as a sauce.

Small caramel custards can be made in dariole molds. Cook for about 20 min.

6 servings

CUSTARD PIE

3 tbs. cornstarch	A little grated
1 qt. milk	nutmeg
3 eggs	Shortcrust
3 tbs. sugar	Pastry using
	1½ cups flour, etc.

Blend the cornstarch with a little of the cold milk and boil the rest of the milk. Pour the boiling milk onto the blended cornstarch, stirring well. Return to pan, reboil 2-3 min.; remove from heat. Work together the eggs and sugar; when the cornstarch mixture is cooler, add this to the worked eggs.

Line a 9-in. flan ring or a shallow glass baking dish with Shortcrust Pastry, and prick the base. Pour in the custard mixture, dust with a little grated nutmeg, if liked, and bake in a fairly hot oven (190 °C, 375 °F) until the pastry is browned, then reduce the heat to 175 °C, 335 °F, until the custard is set — 45 min.

QUEEN OF PUDDINGS

2½ cups milk	2 eggs
1¼ cups bread	3 tbs. jam
crumbs	½-¾ cup
4 tbs. butter *or*	sugar
margarine	
Grated rind of 2	
lemons	

Heat the milk and add the bread crumbs, butter, lemon rind, and ¼ cup sugar. Let soak for 30 min. Separate the eggs and stir the yolks into the milk mixture. Pour the mixture into a buttered baking dish and bake for about ¾ hr. in a moderate oven (180 °C, 350 °F) until set. Now spread the jam on the pudding. Whip the egg whites,

sprinkle with 2 tbs. sugar, and whip again until stiff. Then lightly fold in the rest of the sugar. Spread the meringue over the pudding and put into a very cool oven (130 °C, 265 °F) until the top is set and golden brown.

5 – 6 servings

QUEEN'S PUDDING

2½ cups cookie or	Vanilla extract
cake crumbs	6-9 apricot
2½ cups milk	halves, canned *or*
¼ cup sugar	bottled
2 eggs	Glacé cherries

Apricot Sauce:

1¼ cups apricot	1 tbs. kirsch
syrup	*or* rum
Sugar to taste	

Rub the crumbs through a fine sieve or use a blender. Heat the milk, add the crumbs, let stand for 10-15 min., until soft, then beat until smooth. Beat in the sugar and eggs. Flavor with the vanilla. Grease a plain mold or bowl with butter, line the base with a round of greased paper, and sprinkle with sugar. Pour in the mixture and cover with paper. Stand the mold in a pan of hot water and bake in a warm oven (170 °C, 335 ° F) until the mixture is firm; this takes about 1 hr.

While the pudding cooks, make the sauce by boiling the apricot syrup, with sugar added to taste, until it is slightly reduced. Use the syrup from the can or bottle for this. Add the kirsch or rum after reducing it.

When the pudding is set in the middle, let it stand for a few min., then carefully unmold onto a dish. Tear off the paper, arrange the apricot halves around the dish, decorate the pudding with the cherries, and pour the Apricot Sauce around it.

6 servings

Soufflés and Omelets

HOT SOUFFLÉS, TO MAKE

Soufflés depend for their lightness on the air beaten into the egg whites they contain. They must not get wet or be jolted to knock the air out, and they should be served as soon as they are removed from the oven, as they fall as soon as they cool.

General Hints

1) Before making a soufflé, prepare the pan or mold (see below) and turn on the steamer or oven.

2) When making, beat the egg whites very stiff, incorporating as much bulk of air as possible by lifting the beater or whisk in a rotating movement. Fold them into the soufflé very carefully. Cook immediately.

3) Time the preparation and cooking so that the soufflé *can* be served as soon as it is cooked.

To prepare the pan or mold Grease with clarified butter or cooking fat. Tie a double band of waxed paper or aluminum foil around the container, to rise 3 in. above the top. (The cut edge of paper should be at the top.) For a steamed soufflé, cut a circle of waxed paper for the top of the pan to prevent water dripping onto the soufflé.

Steamed Soufflés These are cooked in a steamer or

Custards come in many guises

9

saucepan containing enough boiling water to come halfway up the sides of the pan. Stand the soufflé dish on an upturned saucer or plate so that it does not touch the bottom of the pan itself. Only half-fill the mold. Steam gently but steadily, avoiding jolting the pan. The soufflé is cooked when it is just risen and firm to the touch. Turn out onto a hot dish and serve at once.

Baked Soufflés These are served in the cooking dish, usually a large charlotte or soufflé mold, or in individual casserole dishes. The greased dish should not be more than ¾ full. Avoid opening the oven door during cooking, so that no cold draft or jolting can make the soufflé sink.

VANILLA SOUFFLÉ (Basic Soufflé)

3 tbs. butter	3 tbs. sugar
⅜ cup flour	½ tsp. vanilla
1 cup milk	extract
4 egg yolks	5 egg whites

Prepare the soufflé mold according to the cooking method to be used, as described under Hot Soufflés. Melt the butter, stir in the flour, and cook gently for a few min. without coloring. Add the warmed milk; stir well until smooth. Reheat, stirring continuously, until the mixture thickens and begins to leave the sides of the pan. Let cool. Beat in the egg yolks, sugar, and vanilla extract. Beat the egg whites stiffly and fold them in gently. Pour the mixture into the mold and cover it. Steam for ¾-1 hr., or bake in a fairly hot oven (190 °C, 375 °F) for 30-35 min.

Variations

Ginger Soufflé Replace the flour with ¼ cup cornstarch mixed to a paste with a little of the milk. Use ⅝ cup milk, 4 tbs. butter, 4 tbs. sugar, and ⅝ cup syrup from preserved ginger. Flavor with 6 tbs. chopped preserved ginger.
Lemon or Orange Soufflé Use 1 cup milk, 5 egg yolks, and 6 whites. Flavor with the finely grated rind of 1½ lemons or oranges and 2 tsp. lemon or orange juice.

6 servings

CHOCOLATE SOUFFLÉ

¼ cup finely	4 egg yolks
grated plain	⅜ cup sugar
chocolate	½ tsp. vanilla
1 cup milk	extract
2 tbs. butter	5 egg whites
⅜ cup flour	

Prepare a soufflé dish or mold. Dissolve the chocolate in the milk. Melt the butter; add the flour and let it cook for a few min. without coloring. Add the milk and beat well until smooth. Reheat until the mixture thickens and comes away from the sides of the pan. Allow to cool slightly. Beat in the egg yolks well, 1 at a time; add the sugar and vanilla extract. Beat the egg whites until stiff and fold them lightly into the mixture. Turn into the mold; cover and steam very gently for about 1 hr.

6 servings

SWEET OMELETS, TO MAKE

1) Sweet omelets can be flat, or puffed like a soufflé by beating the egg whites separately and folding them into the rest of the mixture.
2) The pan should be the right size for the number of eggs; a 2-egg omelet needs a 6-in. diameter pan. Ideally, the pan should be kept only for omelets and should be cleaned only with a dry cloth and a little salt.
3) A palette knife or spatula is useful for

folding omelets.
4) Take care not to overcook an omelet and make it tough; cook it until the top is just set. A puffed or soufflé omelet may need finishing under the broiler. All omelets should be served as soon as they are made.

Basic Sweet Omelet and Fillings

2 eggs	1 tbs. sugar
Pinch of salt	1 tbs. unsalted
1 tbs. cream	butter

Beat the eggs thoroughly with the salt, cream, and sugar. Heat the butter in an omelet pan and remove any scum. When the butter is really hot, pour in the omelet mixture and stir until it begins to set. Lift the edge nearest the pan handle. Fold it over to rest on the edge farthest from the handle. Tip the folded omelet out onto a hot dish. Dredge with sugar and serve at once.

Any Sweet Filling can be added, such as warmed jam, fruit puree, or diced soft fruit. It should be spread evenly in the center of the omelet just before folding it.

For a Rum Omelet, add 1 tbs. rum to the egg mixture. Pour 1 tbs. warmed rum around the completed omelet, and light it.

2 servings

CHOCOLATE SOUFFLÉ OMELET
For the Sauce and Filling:

¼ cup cocoa	2 tbs. apricot
3 tbs. brown	jam
sugar	2 tbs. butter
⅝ cup milk	

For the Omelet:

2 large eggs	1 tbs. rum
2 tbs. sugar	1 tbs. butter

Make the sauce. Place all the sauce ingredients in a saucepan; dissolve the sugar over low heat, then bring the mixture to a boil, stirring continuously. Cook for about 5 min., until smooth and shiny. Keep warm over hot water until needed.

To make the omelet, separate the yolks and whites. Beat the yolks with the sugar until light, trickle in the rum, and beat until pale and light. Beat the egg whites until stiff, and fold them into the mixture. Melt the butter in a heavy frying pan about 7 in. in diameter. Do not allow it to brown. Pour the egg mixture into the pan, and cook over low heat, stirring occasionally, until the underside is brown. Brown the top for a few min. under a hot broiler.

Pour some of the chocolate sauce into the center of the omelet, fold it over carefully, and turn it onto a hot plate. Serve immediately, with the extra sauce separately.

2-3 servings

ONE-EGG OMELET, SAVORY OR SWEET

½-1 tbs. butter	1 egg
Seasoning	

Heat the butter in an omelet pan. Add the seasoned and beaten egg. When just beginning to set, push back egg mixture so only ½ pan is covered. Cook quickly, allowing liquid egg to flow down sides of pan. Put in filling — if the omelet is not to be served plain — fold away from pan handle, and tip onto a hot plate. Serve at once, garnished with a sauce.
The following fillings are to be recommended:
Creamed Custard Cook a small quantity of custard, sieve, then reheat with a little butter and cream. Season well.
Creamed Cake Heat cubes of firm cake in a sweetened white sauce.
Cheese Fill with sweetened cream cheese before folding.
Jam Fill with warmed jam as desired.
Fruit Fill with a stiff puree of sweetened stewed fruit.

Batter Puddings, Pancakes, and Fritters

SWEET BATTER MIXTURES

Sweet batters, baked, steamed, or fried, are made from flour, milk, and eggs, with a pinch each of sugar and salt for flavoring. They are beaten together, using only half the liquid at first, until well-blended and smooth.

The lightness of any batter depends on steam forming quickly within the mixture and on the flour cooking quickly. Bake a batter in a hot oven (220 °C, 425 °F) at first; reduce the heat to 190 °C, 375 °F, to finish cooking.

To steam a batter, prepare a mold in the same way as for a steamed pudding, and use the same method (*see* Steamed and Boiled Puddings).

Batters are most often fried to make pancakes or as a coating for fritters.

BATTER PUDDING
(Basic — baked or steamed)

2 cups flour	1 tbs. cooking
¼ tsp. each sugar	fat *or* lard
and salt	Wine, syrup, *or*
2½ cups milk	jam sauce

Sift the flour, sugar, and salt into a bowl. Make a well in the center of the flour and break the eggs into this. Add about ⅝ cup of the milk. Stir, gradually working the flour down from the sides and adding more milk, as required, to make a stiff batter consistency. Beat well for about 5 min. Add the rest of the milk. Cover and let stand. Put the fat into a Yorkshire pudding pan and heat in the oven until hot. The fat should be just beginning to smoke. Quickly pour in the batter and cook in a hot oven (220 °C, 425 °F) at the top of the oven until nicely browned. Reduce the heat to 190 °C, 375 °F, and cook through, for 10-15 min. Serve with wine, syrup, or jam sauce.

For a steamed Batter Pudding, prepare the same mixture. Pour it into a well-greased pudding dish. Cover with greased paper and steam for 2 hr.

6 servings

Batter Pudding with Apples

Pancakes

BATTER PUDDING WITH APPLES

2 cups flour	¼ cup sugar
¼ tsp. each sugar and salt	¼ tsp. ground cinnamon *or*
2 eggs	grated lemon rind
2½ cups milk	1 tbs. butter
3 medium apples	

Prepare the batter as for Batter Pudding. Cover and let stand for 30 min. Core, peel, and slice the apples thinly. Sprinkle them with the sugar and cinnamon or lemon rind. Spread them over a well-greased bowl or pudding dish. Pour the batter over, flake the butter on top, and bake in a hot oven (220 °C, 425 °F) until brown, 20-25 min. Reduce the heat to 190 °C, 375 °F, and finish cooking. Dredge with sugar before serving.

For **Batter Pudding with Dried Fruit,** substitute ¾ cup mixed dried fruit for the apples.
6 servings   Cooking time – 30-40 min.

PANCAKES

Batter as for Batter Pudding above	A little cooking fat
	1 lemon
	Sugar

Put about ½ tbs. of cooking fat into a clean frying pan and heat until it is just beginning to smoke. Quickly pour in enough batter to coat thinly the bottom of the pan, tilting the pan to make sure the batter runs over evenly. More the frying pan over a quick heat until the pancake is set and browned underneath. Make sure the pancake is loose at the sides, then toss, or turn with a spatula. Brown on the other side and turn onto a sugared paper. Sprinkle with sugar and lemon juice, roll up, and keep hot while cooking the rest. Serve dredged with sugar and pieces of cut lemon.

Other flavorings, such as apple, jam, orange, tangerine, or brandy may be used, as follows:
Apple Pancakes Add grated lemon rind to the batter. Fill with apple puree mixed with seedless raisins and a little lemon juice.
Jam Pancakes Spread with jam before rolling up.
Orange Pancakes Make the pancakes, but sprinkle with orange juice and serve with pieces of cut orange.
Tangerine Pancakes Add grated tangerine rind to the batter. Sprinkle with tangerine juice before rolling up.
Brandy Filling for Pancakes Cream together 4 tbs. butter and 2 tbs. sugar until soft. Work in 1 tbs. brandy and 1 tsp. lemon juice. Spread the pancakes with this mixture. Roll up and put immediately into the serving dish.

CREPES SUZETTE

1¼ cups batter as for Batter Pudding above	Confectioners' sugar
	Brandy *or* rum

Filling:

4 tbs. butter	1 tsp. lemon juice
⅜ cup sugar	1 tbs. kirsch
Grated rind of ½ orange	*or* curaçao
2 tsp. orange juice	

Make the batter and let stand. Cream together the butter and sugar for the filling until very soft. Then work in the orange juice, rind, lemon juice, and liqueur. Make a very thin pancake, spread with some filling, roll up, and dredge with confectioners' sugar. Put into a warm place while making and filling the rest of the pancakes. Just before serving, pour the warmed brandy or rum over the pancakes and light it. Serve immediately.

If you prefer, warm the filling with the brandy until liquid, and pour it over the unfilled pancakes folded over twice. Light and serve.

COATING BATTERS FOR SWEET FRITTERS (Light)

½ cup flour	2 tsp. salad
Pinch each of	oil *or* oiled butter
sugar and salt	5 tbs. warm water
	1 egg white

Sift together the flour and salt. Mix to a smooth consistency with the oil and water. Beat well, and let stand for 30 min. Just before using, beat the egg white until stiff and fold it into the batter.

(Rich)

1 cup flour	1 egg
Pinch each of	⅝ cup milk
sugar and salt	

Sift together the flour and salt. Make a well in the center of the flour and add the egg and some of the milk. Mix to a stiff consistency, using more milk if required. Beat well. Add the rest of the milk. Let stand for about 30 min.

For a batter for loose mixtures, *see* Indian Fritters.

SWEET FRITTERS

1) Most fritters are made with batter, used as a coating or to make a mixture stick together. Some batters contain beaten egg whites, others yeast, beer, or brandy. Some are sweetened or flavored with liqueurs or spices.

2) The fritters can be deep-fried, or shallow-fried in fat at least 1-in deep. The fat must be hot enough to seal the batter instantly, about 375 °F. At the correct temperature a drop of batter will sink, rise to the surface at once, and then begin to color.

3) Lower fritters gently into the hot fat, using a slotted spoon if you can. Turn and withdraw them in the same way. Place a frying basket, if used, in the fat *before* putting in the fritters, so that they are sealed by the hot fat before touching it.

4) Only fry a few fritters at a time, and let the undersides brown before turning them. Turn once only. Let the fat reheat when you take out the fritters, while you drain them on absorbent paper. Keep warm until all fritters are made. Dust with sugar just before serving.

Variations

Apple Fritters 2 apples, cored and sliced; coating batter; sugar for dredging; lemon wedges; and lemon hard sauce.

Apricot Fritters Canned apricot halves, drained; coating batter; sugar mixed with ground cinnamon for dredging.

Banana Fritters 4 firm bananas, cut lengthwise and across; coating batter; sugar for dredging.

Bread-and-Butter Fritters 6 thin jam sandwiches without crusts; coating batter; sugar mixed with ground cinnamon for dredging.

Orange Fritters 4 oranges, peeled and without pith, in pieces of 3-4 segments; coating batter; sugar for dredging.

Pineapple Fritters 8-10 canned pineapple rings, drained; coating batter; sugar for dredging. Use the syrup from the can for a sauce.

BEIGNETS OR SOUFFLÉ FRITTERS

1 cup flour	3 large eggs
Pinch of salt	Vanilla extract
1¼ cups water	Fat for deep
½ cup butter *or*	frying
margarine	Sugar

Make Choux Pastry: sift the flour and salt. Put the water and fat in a saucepan and, when the fat has melted, bring to boiling point. Add the sifted flour all at once and beat well over the heat until the mixture leaves the sides of the pan — about 1 min. Allow to cool slightly and add the beaten eggs gradually and then vanilla extract to taste, beating well. Heat the deep fat until it is just beginning to haze. Grease a dessertspoon and, with it, drop small spoonfuls of the pastry into the fat. Cook gently until crisp and lightly browned. Drain well. Dredge with sugar and serve hot.

Note: It is advisable to test a fritter from each batch to ensure that the center is cooked, since the time for cooking depends on the temperature of the fat.

5-6 servings   Cooking time – 7-10 min.

INDIAN FRITTERS

¾ cup flour	2 egg yolks
Pinch of salt	Frying-fat
Boiling water	Jam *or* jelly
2 eggs	

Sift the flour into a bowl with a pinch of salt. Stir in a good ¼ cup of boiling water and beat to form a very stiff smooth paste. Let cool slightly. Beat in the eggs and egg yolks gradually and thoroughly. Have ready a deep fat, heated to 375 °F. Half-fill a tablespoon with the mixture and put a teaspoon of jam or jelly in the center; cover with more of the batter mixture; drop this into the hot fat. Cook until golden brown, about 3 min. Drain well. Dredge with sugar or serve with a sauce made from the same jam or jelly as the filling.

5-6 servings   Cooking time – 15-20 min.

Apple Fritters

Pies, Tarts and Pastry Puddings

All these use pastry of one kind or another, so the most usual types of pastry are described here, before the recipes for the dishes themselves. Since the traditional suet puddings in the next section also use pastry, the recipe for suet-crust pastry is included here, as is the recipe for Choux Pastry, because, although used mostly for cold desserts, gâteaux, and pastries such as éclairs, hot sweet (and savory) puffs, or Choux, can make very useful "containers" for various fillings or stuffings.

The aim in making any pastry is to make a crust as light as possible. This depends on the amount of cold air trapped in the pastry when making it. In puff or flaky pastry, the air is trapped between thin layers of dough. In shortcrust and similar pastry, the air is held in a myriad of tiny spaces throughout the pastry.

Frozen shortcrust or puff pastry, in a block or already shaped, is quite satisfactory for most of the dishes below. A pastry mix in a package will also do, with the added advantage that flavorings or egg yolk can be added to make the pastry spicier or richer than usual.

Pastry trimmings, especially of puff pastry, can be well-used for fritters and for small decorative cookies to accompany desserts such as ice creams. They can also be used for jam tartlets.

PASTRY-MAKING HINTS

Ingredients

You can use only self-rising flour for plain shortcrust pastry and suet-crust pastry. Use plain flour for all rich and sweetened pastry.

Butter, or butter mixed with lard or shortening, should be used if possible. When the amount of fat is less than half the amount of flour, add a little baking powder (1 level tsp. to 2 cups flour).

When making the pastry

1) Sift the flour and any sugar used.
2) Use only your fingertips when rubbing fat into flour. Lift your hands high, so that air is caught up as the flour falls back into the bowl.
3) Use chilled water for mixing, and mix with a round-bladed knife. Do not use more water than you need; it will made the pastry hard.
4) Handle the pastry little and lightly. Let puff and flaky pastry "stand" for 15 min. between every 2 rollings. *All* pastry should stand in a cool place after being made, for at least 15 min.
5) Roll pastry lightly and evenly, with short strokes, in one direction only. Lift the rolling pin just short of the edge so as not to squeeze air out.
6) Use very little flour for rolling out. Remove any extra with a pastry brush. Occasionally, pastry is rolled on sugar, or sugar is rolled into the surface before baking. Keep the board cool and your hands dry, and sweep off any surplus.
7) The richer the pastry, the hotter the oven you need. If it is not hot enough, the melted fat runs out and leaves the pastry hard and tough. It also wastes fat.

To glaze pastry for sweet dishes

Fruit tarts, puffs, etc. can be brushed lightly with cold water and dredged with sugar before being baked. If a thin coating of icing is wanted, they can be brushed with well-beaten egg white and dredged with sugar when nearly baked.

CHOUX PASTRY (For soufflé fritters, cream puffs, profiteroles, etc.)

1 cup flour	½ tsp. vanilla
1¼ cups water	extract
⅛ tsp. salt	1 egg yolk
4 tbs. butter *or*	2 eggs
margarine	

Sift and warm the flour. Place water, salt, and butter in a pan and bring to boiling point. Remove from heat, add flour all at once, and beat well over the heat again, until it becomes a smooth soft paste and leaves the sides of the pan clean. Remove from the heat, add vanilla and egg yolk immediately, and beat well. Add the other 2 eggs 1 at a time, beating thoroughly between each addition. (It is important to get the first of the egg in while the mixture is hot enough to cook it slightly, otherwise it becomes too soft.) Add any flavoring last. Use while tepid. Bake in a fairly hot oven (200 °C, 400 °F). Do not underbake.

CRUMB PASTRY

Crumb pastry can provide a useful shortcut to making a tart shell or piecrust. It is made with bread crumbs, toast, cookie crumbs, or cornflakes. The materials are crushed by hand, wrapped in a cloth, and rolled with a rolling pin, or are processed in an electric blender. As a rule, 3¾ cups crumbs combined with 6 tbs. melted butter are used, with sugar and spice flavoring to taste. This should make a shell for an 8-in. plate tart. Mix well the crumbs with the butter, and press firmly into the bottom and sides of the plate. Either chill and then fill with a custard or firm fruit puree, or chill and then bake at 180 °C, 350 °F, for 15 min.

Fatty crumbs may need less butter; whole meal stale bread crumbs may need a little more. A luxury crust can be obtained by using gingersnaps or graham crackers for the crumbs, or the following mixture.

2 cups cookie	⅝ cup melted
crumbs	butter
6 tbs. unblanched	⅓ tsp. cinnamon
ground almonds	
5 tbs. thin cream	

PÂTÉ SUCRÉE OR SWEET PASTRY

2 cups flour	¼ cup sugar
Pinch of salt	1 egg yolk
⅝ cup butter	Cold water to mix

Sift together the flour and salt. Cut the butter into small pieces and rub it lightly into the flour, using your fingertips. Add the sugar, and mix with egg yolk and sufficient cold water to make a stiff paste. Use as required.

In warm weather only a very small quantity of water will be required.

PUFF PASTRY

4 cups flour	1 tsp. lemon
Pinch of salt	juice
1 lb. butter	¾ cup cold water
	(approx.)

Sift the flour and salt and rub in about 4 tbs. of butter. Press the remaining butter firmly in a floured cloth to remove the moisture, and shape into a flat cake. Add the lemon juice to the flour, and mix to a smooth dough with cold water. The consistency of the dough must be the same as that of the butter. Knead the dough well, and roll it into a strip a little wider than the butter and somewhat more than twice its length. Place the butter on ½ of the pastry, fold the other ½ over, and press the edges together with a rolling pin to form a neat parcel. Leave in a cool place for 15 min. to allow the butter to harden.

Roll out into a long strip 3 times the original length but the original width, keeping the corners square and the sides straight to ensure an even thickness when the pastry is folded. Do not let the butter break through the dough. Fold the bottom third up and the top third down; press the edges together with a rolling pin; and half turn the pastry, so that the folded edges are on the right and left. Roll and fold again and lay aside in a cool place for 15 min. Repeat this process until the pastry has been rolled out 6 times. The rolling should be done as evenly as possible, and the pastry kept in a long narrow shape which, when folded, forms a square. Roll

Stages in making shortcrust pastry
Left: Sifting the flour into a bowl
Middle: Rubbing in the fat
Right: Gathering the dough into shape

out as required and leave in a cool place. Bake in a very hot oven (230 °C, 450 °F). The oven door should not be opened until the pastry has risen and become partly baked, as a current of cold air may cause the pastry to collapse.

SHORT AND RICH SHORTCRUST PASTRY FOR PIES, TARTS, ETC.

FOR STANDARD SHORTCRUST PASTRY

2 cups flour	4 tbs. butter *or*
Pinch each of	margarine
sugar and salt	4 tbs. lard
	Cold water to mix

Sift the flour, sugar, and salt together. Rub the fats into the flour, using only the fingertips. Mix to a stiff paste with cold water.

FOR RICH SHORTCRUST PASTRY

2 cups flour	1 tsp. sugar
½-¾ cup butter	1 egg yolk
(sweet cream	Cold water to mix
type, if possible)	(about 1 tbs.)

Make as above, on a flat surface rather than in a bowl. Before adding water, make a well in the dry ingredients and put in the egg yolk. Sprinkle with the sugar, and mix with fingertips or a knife. Add the water as required, and mix.

SUET-CRUST PASTRY

⅜-½ cup suet	1 tsp. baking
2 cups flour	powder
¼ tsp. salt	Cold water to mix

Chop the suet finely (or use ready-shredded suet). Sift the flour, salt, and baking powder, and mix in the suet. Mix to a firm dough with cold water.

PIES, FLANS, AND TARTS, TO MAKE

Some pies have only a pastry crust on top. Others are made in a pastry shell lining the pie plate or dish and have a top crust or lattice of pastry as well. They are sometimes called Double Crust Pies.

The method of lining a pie plate or dish with pastry is described under Open and Double Crust Pies and Tarts, as is the method of putting on a top crust or covering of pastry. Another way of putting on a top crust is described under Fruit Pies and Tarts.

Open and Double-Crust Pies and Tarts

Open tarts are usually baked on oven-proof glass or enamel plates. The tarts can be filled with jam, syrup, molasses, custard, fruit, etc. You will need about 4 oz. pastry (i.e. 1 cup flour plus other ingredients) for a 7-in. plate.

20

Lining a flan ring

Knead the pastry into a round shape. Then roll it into a circle about ⅛ in. thick and a little larger than the plate. Fold the pastry over the rolling pin and gently lift it onto the plate. Smooth it over the surface carefully, making sure that there are no air bubbles underneath. Do not stretch the pastry in lifting or smoothing it, as it will shrink back later.

If the tart is to be partly or wholly baked before being filled, prick the bottom with a fork, and bake it. Bake according to the type of pastry. Stand the plate on a baking sheet in the oven.

You can give the tart a lattice top made of strips of pastry, or decorate the edge with fancy shapes.

Double crust pies and tarts are usually shallow like open tarts, and are baked on similar plates. You will need about 8 oz.

pastry (i.e. 2 cups flour plus other ingredients) for an 8-in. plate.

Divide the dough into 2 parts. Form each into a round shape. Roll out 1 part into a circle and use it to line the plate or dish as described above.

Put in a layer of filling, sprinkle with sugar if you wish, and cover with another layer of filling. This prevents the sugar getting into the pastry and making it soggy.

Roll out the remaining piece of pastry into a circle a little larger than the plate. Lift onto the rolling pin, and lay the pastry in position on the pie without stretching it. Pinch or press the top and bottom edges of pastry together, flute the edge with the back of a fork, and decorate the top if you wish.

Bake according to the type of pastry, with the plate standing on a baking sheet.

21

To line a flan ring

To line a 7-in. flan ring, about 4 oz. pastry (i.e. 1 cup flour plus the other ingredients made into pastry) will be required. Grease a baking sheet and the flan ring; place the flan ring on the baking sheet. Roll the pastry into a circle about 1 in. larger than the flan ring and ⅛ in. thick. Lift the pastry with the rolling pin to prevent stretching, and line the ring carefully with the pastry. Press to fit the bottom and sides so that no air bubbles form underneath the crust. Trim off the surplus pastry with a sharp knife or roll across the top of the ring with a rolling pin.

Baking "blind"

First line the unbaked pastry shell of an open tart or flan with waxed paper. Fill this with dried beans, rice, or pasta. Bake according to the type of pastry until the shell is partly or fully baked, as the recipe requires. Remove it from the oven, and take out the dried filling (you can use this over and over again) and the paper. Return the shell to the oven for 4-5 min. to dry the inside of the lining. Cover with buttered waxed paper if getting too brown.

Fruit pies and tarts

An 8-in. pie dish will require about 6 oz. pastry (i.e. 1½ cups flour plus the other ingredients made into pastry) and 1½-2 lb. fruit.

Place ½ the amount of fruit in the dish, sprinkle over the sugar and flavoring, if used, and pile the remaining fruit on top, piling it high in the center. The sugar should not be sprinkled on top as it would go into the pastry and make it soggy. If the fruit is likely to shrink during cooking, or if there is insufficient fruit to fill the dish, place a pie funnel or inverted eggcup in the center.

Roll out the pastry a little larger than the pie dish. Cut off a strip of pastry the width and length of the rim of the dish, wet the edge of the pie dish with cold water, and place the strip on the pie dish cut edge inward, without stretching it. Join the strip by wetting the cut ends and pressing them firmly together.

Wet the strip of pastry; lift the remaining pastry with the rolling pin; place it gently over the dish, taking care not to stretch it. Press the strip and the cover together and trim off the surplus with a sharp knife. Flute the edge of the pastry with the back of a fork or decorate to your fancy.

To allow the steam to escape, either cut a slit in the center of the crust before placing pie in the oven (if a pie funnel has been used, the slit should come over it), *or* leave a few gaps under the pastry cover at the edge, *or* raise the pastry slightly at 1 corner immediately after cooking.

APPLE PIE

Shortcrust pastry using 1½ cups flour, etc. 4-6 medium apples	½ cup moist sugar 6 cloves *or* ½ tsp. grated lemon rind

Peel, quarter, and core the apples, and cut in thick slices. Place ½ the apples in an 8-in. pie dish; add the sugar and flavoring; pile the remaining fruit on top, piling it high in the center. Line the edge of the pie dish with pastry, and cover the pie with pastry. Flute the edges of the pastry with the back of a fork. Bake for 40 min., first in a fairly hot oven (200 °C, 400 °F), reducing the heat to moderate (180 °C, 350 °F) when the pastry is set. Dredge with sugar and serve hot or cold.

Use the same method for other fruit pies, such as damson, blueberry, or peach pie.

6 servings

APPLE AND RAISIN LATTICE OR CHEESE TART

Shortcrust pastry, frozen *or* using 2 cups flour, etc. 1 tart dessert apple 1½ cups seedless raisins	1 tbs. lemon juice ½-¾ cup sugar, brown *or* white 2 tbs. flour Pinch of salt 2 tbs. butter

Line a 9-in. pie plate with ⅔ pastry, reserving the rest for lattice strips. Peel, core, and chop apple, and toss in lemon juice to coat. Mix the fruits, then mix in any dry ingredients. Turn into the pastry-lined plate. Dot with butter and arrange a lattice of pastry strips over the top. Bake in a very hot oven (230 °C, 450 °F) for 7-8 min., then reduce heat to moderate (180 °C, 350 °F) for 30-40 min.

If you prefer, cover the tart with a crumble of cottage cheese, grated cheddar cheese, and fine white soft bread crumbs before baking, and dredge with confectioners' sugar afterward.

APRICOT TART

Shortcrust pastry, using 1½ cups flour, etc.	1 14-15-oz. can of apricots Sugar to taste

Place the apricots in an 8-in. pie dish; sprinkle with sugar; half-fill the dish with the syrup from the can. Line the edge of the dish with pastry, cover with the remaining pastry, and bake in a fairly hot oven (200 °C, 400 °F) for 30-40 min. When the pastry has set, brush it lightly with water and dredge well with sugar. Return to oven quickly and finish cooking.

6 servings

BAKEWELL TART

Shortcrust pastry, using 1 cup flour, etc. Raspberry jam 4 tbs. butter 4 tbs. sugar 1 egg	½ cup ground almonds 1¼ cups cake crumbs Almond extract Confectioners' sugar

Line a 7-in. flan ring or pie plate with the pastry. Place a good layer of raspberry jam on the bottom. Cream together the butter and sugar until thick and white. Beat in the egg and add the ground almonds, cake crumbs, and a few drops of almond extract. Spread the mixture on top of the jam and bake in a fairly hot oven (200 °C, 400 °F) for about ½ hr. Sprinkle confectioners' sugar on top and serve hot or cold.

5-6 servings

FRANGIPANE TART

Rich shortcrust pastry, using 1 cup flour, etc. ¼ cup sugar 4 tbs. butter	1 egg ½ cup ground almonds 1 tsp. flour

Line a 7-in. flan ring or pie plate with the pastry. Cream the butter and sugar until thick and white. Add the egg, beating well, then mix in the ground almonds and flour. Place the mixture in the pastry shell and bake in a moderate oven (180 °C, 350 °F) for 25-30 min. When cool, dredge with confectioners' sugar.

6 servings

PRUNE TART

Shortcrust pastry using 1½ cups flour, etc. 2 cups prunes	2 tbs. cranberry juice Sugar to taste

Soak the prunes, remove the stones, and take out the kernels. Put the fruit and kernels in the cranberry juice, add sugar, and simmer for 10 min. Allow to cool; place in an 8-in. pie dish. Line the edge of the dish with pastry and cover with remaining pastry. Bake for about 45 min. in a fairly hot oven (200 °C, 400 °F). Dredge with sugar and serve.

6 servings

MOLASSES TART

Shortcrust pastry using 1½ cups flour, etc. 3 tbs. light corn syrup	Lemon juice *or* ginger 1¼ cups fresh bread crumbs

Slightly warm the syrup, flavor with a pinch of ginger or a little lemon juice, then stir in the bread crumbs.

Line a 9-in. oven-proof plate with the pastry; trim and decorate the edge. Spread with the syrup mixture, decorate with cross strips of pastry, and bake in a fairly hot oven (200 °C, 400 °F) for about 30 min.

Note: If preferred, the tart may be baked as a double-crust tart: increase the amount of pastry and bake for 50 min. Crushed

Cheese-Topped Apple Tart

cornflakes can be substituted for the bread crumbs.

6 servings

MINCE PIES

Shortcrust, rich	10-12 oz.
shortcrust *or*	mincemeat
puff pastry, using	Granulated *or*
1½ cups flour,	confectioners'
etc.	sugar

Roll the pastry out to about ⅛-in. thickness. Cut ½ of it into rounds about 2½-in. diameter and reserve these for lids. (Use a plain cutter for flaky, rough puff, or puff pastry.) Cut the remaining pastry into rounds of about 3-in. diameter and line

some patty shell pans. Place some mincemeat in the pans, brush the edge of the pastry with water, and place a lid on top of each. Press the edges together well; if a plain cutter has been used, flute the edges. Brush the tops with water, and sprinkle with sugar. Make a hole or 2 small cuts in the top of each. Bake in a hot oven (220 °C-230 °C, 425 °F-450 °F) depending on the type of pastry, for 25-30 min. Dredge tops with granulated *or* confectioners' sugar. Serve hot or cold.

8-10 pies

Apple Dumplings, baked and glazed

Apple Pie

ALMOND PUDDING

Shortcrust pastry using 1 cup flour, etc.	1¼ cups cake *or* white bread crumbs
6 tbs. butter	½ lemon
¼ cup sugar	¾ cup ground almonds
2 eggs	2½ cups milk

Line the sides of an 8-in. pie dish with pastry. Cream the butter and sugar together; beat in the eggs gradually. Add the crumbs, lemon rind, juice, and almonds. Boil the milk; pour it over the rest of the mixture into the lined pie dish. Bake in a moderate to fairly hot oven (180-190 °C, 350-375 °F) until the pastry is cooked and the filling is golden brown and set, about 20-30 min.

6-7 servings

APPLE AMBER

Shortcrust pastry	4 tbs. butter
4 medium cooking apples	⅜ cup brown sugar
2 tbs. water	2 eggs
Rind of 1 lemon	¼-⅜ cup sugar

Line the sides of an 8-in. pie dish with the pastry and decorate the edge.

Peel, core, and slice the apples; put them in a saucepan and stew with the water and the lemon rind. When soft, pass through a nylon sieve. Return the apple pulp to the pan and reheat slightly; add the butter, brown sugar, and egg yolks. Put the mixture into the lined pie dish and bake gently in a moderate oven (180 °C, 350 °F) for about 30 min., until the apple mixture is set. Stiffly beat the egg whites and fold in ¼-⅜ cup of sugar. Pile on top of the apple mixture, dredge lightly with sugar, and decorate, if liked, with pieces of angelica and glacé cherry. Bake in a very cool oven (150 °C, 290 °F) until the meringue is golden brown — about 30-40 min. Serve hot or cold.

Note: A good pinch of ground cinnamon and ground cloves can be added to the apples before the butter, sugar, and egg yolks, if liked.

6-7 servings

APPLE DUMPLINGS

Shortcrust pastry, using 3 cups flour for large apples *or* 2 cups flour for small apples	A little grated lemon rind *or* ground cinnamon
	6 cooking apples
	12 cloves
¼ cup brown sugar	(optional)

Make the shortcrust pastry; divide into 6 portions, shaping each into a round.

Mix the sugar and grated lemon rind or cinnamon. Peel and core each apple and put it on a round of pastry. Work the pastry around the apple until it is almost covered. Press the cloves, if used, into the centers of the apples; then fill the cavity with the sugar mixture. Seal the pastry edges by moistening slightly with water. Place the dumplings sealed end down on a greased baking sheet. Brush them with milk and dredge with sugar. Bake for about 30 min. in a fairly hot oven (200 °C, 400 °F).

6 servings

Steamed, Boiled, and Baked Hot Puddings

STEAMED AND SIMILAR PUDDINGS, TO MAKE

Ingredients

Using some bread or cake crumbs instead of all flour will make any pudding lighter. Remember to add a good pinch of salt for every 2 cups of flour. You can use self-rising flour if you omit the baking powder.

The fat may be suet, prepared at home or bought shredded and ready to use; or it may be butter, margarine, or white cooking fat, or a mixture. Use granulated sugar, as the crystals dissolve easily.

Making the pudding

Always prepare the container and a waxed paper and foil lid or cover, if needed, before making the pudding. They should be well-greased with unsalted or clarified butter, margarine, or cooking fat. The edges must be wiped clean, to prevent marks on a dish in which a pudding will be served and to stop the cover slipping off.

To make the pudding mixture, sift the flour, salt, and rising agent together. The fat can be worked into the pudding mixture in various ways.

The "chopped-in" method is used for suet, if prepared at home. Remove the skin, gristle, and fibers in the suet. Sprinkle with some of the measured flour, and chop the suet with it finely, adding more flour if the mixture becomes sticky.

Both the "rubbed-in" and the "creaming" methods can be used for all fats. To rub in the fat, sift the flour, salt, and rising agent into a mixing bowl, chop the fat, and rub it in with the fingertips only, raising the hands to trap air in the mixture as it falls into the bowl. Continue until the mixture is like fine bread crumbs. "Creaming" is used for mixtures that contain too much fat to rub in or which contain no flour. Work the fat with a wooden spoon until it is pale and soft, sifting in the sugar gradually. Beat the eggs in a separate bowl before adding them gradually to the butter-sugar mixture. They should be at room temperature: cold eggs curdle easily.

Liquids are usually added to the mixture last, to make it (as a rule) of a "dropping consistency." This means that the mixture just drops from the spoon when it is shaken lightly. A "soft dropping consistency" means that it falls from the spoon easily. A "slack" consistency means that it falls off almost of its own accord.

For a steamed pudding Have the pan of boiling water ready. If you have no steamer, stand the pudding in a saucepan on an old saucer or plate, with water coming halfway up it. Put a tight lid on the pan, and simmer gently. This is "half-steaming."

When a recipe calls for gentle steaming, let the water simmer only. Always "top up" with boiling water, however. For a steamed pudding, only ¾ fill the container.

Cover the pudding mold with greased paper or with foil, to prevent steam getting in. Put the cover on greased side down. Twist the edges under the rim of the mold, or tie them.

After taking the pudding out of the steamer, give it a few moments to shrink before turning it out.

For a boiled pudding Have rapidly boiling water ready, enough to cover the whole pudding. Cover the pudding securely as above.

If you wish, you can boil a pudding in a mold covered with a floured cloth or in a well-floured cloth only. Roly-poly puddings can be rolled in a floured cloth, forming a sausage shape; tie loosely at each end, leaving room for the pudding to swell. If you use a mold, fill it completely.

Put the pudding into fast-boiling water. Then let the water simmer only, but always "top up" with boiling water.

Let the pudding "stand" for a few moments after removing it from the water, to let it shrink.

Note that Christmas Puddings should be given a clean, dry cloth on top after boiling and should then be stored in waxed paper. They must be boiled for at least 1½ hr. longer before serving.

Christmas Pudding

BROWN BREAD AND CHESTNUT PUDDING

½ lb. chestnuts	½ lb. brown bread
1¼ cups milk	(crumbled
4 tbs. butter *or*	and weighed
margarine	afterward)
½ cup brown	3 tbs. almonds
sugar	¾ cup raisins
Pinch of salt	2 eggs

Grease a 5-cup mold. Roast the chestnuts for about 20 min., remove both skins, and simmer the chestnuts in the milk until tender, then beat well. Add the fat, sugar, and salt.

Meanwhile, rub the brown bread through a wire sieve. Blanch and chop the almonds and mix with the raisins. Add the chestnut mixture and well-beaten eggs; mix well. Pour into a greased mold; cover with greased paper. Steam for 2½-3 hr. Serve with Custard or Wine Sauce.

6-7 servings

CASTLE PUDDINGS

½ cup butter	1 cup self-rising
⅝ cup sugar	flour
2 eggs, well-beaten	1 tbs. milk
½ tsp. vanilla	3 tbs. apple puree
extract	⅜ cup raisins

Cream butter and sugar together until light and fluffy. Gradually beat in the eggs, 1 by 1. Stir in vanilla extract. Fold in sifted flour, milk, apple puree, and raisins. Turn into 8 or 9 greased and floured individual molds, and cover with buttered waxed paper. Steam in ¾-in. boiling water for 30-40 min. or until sponge is springy. Turn out onto a warmed serving dish, and serve immediately. Serve with a strawberry jam sauce.

CANARY PUDDING

¾ cup butter *or*	Grated rind of ½
margarine	lemon
¾ cup sugar	1½ cups flour
3 eggs	1 tsp. baking
	powder

Grease a 1-qt. pudding bowl *or* mold.

Cream together the fat and sugar until soft and lighter in color. Beat in the eggs gradually. Add the lemon rind. Lightly stir in the sifted flour and baking powder. Pour into the bowl *or* mold. Cover with a greased paper. Steam 1½ hr. Turn out and serve with Jam sauce.

6 servings

CHOCOLATE PUDDING
(Made with Chocolate)

3 oz. plain	A few drops of
chocolate	vanilla extract
2 tbs. milk	3 eggs
¾ cup butter	1½ cups flour
¾ cup sugar	¾ tsp. baking
	powder

Grease a mold or bowl.

Grate the chocolate and heat with the milk in a small saucepan until dissolved. Cream the butter, sugar, and melted chocolate together. Add a few drops of vanilla extract. Beat in the eggs. Sift in the flour and baking powder and mix to a soft dropping consistency. Pour the mixture into the mold *or* bowl. Steam for 2 hr. Serve with Custard, Chocolate, *or* Sherry Sauce.

6 servings

CHOCOLATE PUDDING
(Made with Cocoa)

2 cups flour	½ cup sugar
1 tsp. baking	¼ cup cocoa
powder	2 eggs
Pinch of salt	Milk to mix
½ cup butter *or*	A few drops of
margarine	vanilla extract

Grease a 5-cup bowl.

Sift together the flour, salt, and baking powder. Rub in the fat. Add the sugar and cocoa. Mix to a soft dropping consistency with the beaten eggs and milk. Add vanilla extract to taste. Put the mixture in the mold; cover. Steam for 2 hr. Serve with Chocolate Sauce.

6 servings

CHRISTMAS PUDDING

¾ cup finely chopped suet	¾ cup moist brown sugar
2 cups raisins, cut in half	⅔ cup chopped candied peel
1 cup currants	Grated rind of 1 lemon
¼ cup whole almonds	2 eggs
¾ cup flour	½ cup brandy, sherry beer *or* fruit juice (optional)
Pinch of salt	
¼ tsp. grated nutmeg	
2 cups bread crumbs	A little milk

Grease 2 1-qt. molds or bowls; finely chop or shred the suet; clean the fruit; blanch, skin, and chop the almonds.

Sift the flour, salt, and nutmeg into a mixing bowl. Add the bread crumbs, suet, sugar, dried fruit, peel, grated lemon rind, and almonds. Beat the eggs well and stir them and the flavoring (if used) into the mixture. Add milk, and mix to a soft dropping consistency. Put the mixture into the bowls; cover; steam for 5-6 hr.

When you want to use a pudding, boil it for 1½ hr. before serving.

CHRISTMAS PUDDING (RICH)

3½ cups raisins	1 tsp. mixed spice
2 cups currants	1 tsp. grated nutmeg
⅜ cup almonds (chopped)	5 cups bread crumbs
1 tsp. ground ginger	1¼ cups finely chopped *or* shredded suet
2 cups flour	
Pinch of salt	

Castle Puddings

Apricot Pudding

2 cups brown sugar	6 eggs
1½ cups mixed finely chopped candied peel	¼ cup beer
	Juice of 1 orange
	½ cup brandy
	1¼ cups milk (approx.)

Grease 3 5-cup pudding molds. Prepare the dried fruit; stone and chop the raisins; chop the nuts.

Sift the flour, salt, spice, ginger, and nutmeg into a mixing bowl. Add the sugar, bread crumbs, suet, fruit, nuts, and candied peel. Beat the eggs well and add the beer, orange juice, and brandy to them; stir this into the dry ingredients, adding enough milk to make the mixture of a soft dropping consistency. Put the mixture into prepared molds. Cover and boil steadily for 6-7 hr. Take the puddings out of the water and cover them with a clean dry cloth and, when cold, store in a cool place until needed.

When needed, boil the puddings for 1½ hr. before serving.

3 puddings (each to give 6 medium servings)

CHRISTMAS PUDDING (ECONOMICAL)

1 apple	1 cup shredded suet *or* finely chopped suet
3 cups mixed dried fruit (currants, raisins)	
	1 cup mixed chopped candied peel
1 cup flour	
¼ cup self-rising flour	Juice and rind of 1 lemon
Pinch of salt	2 eggs
2½ cups bread crumbs	Milk to mix
½ cup moist brown sugar	A little caramel *or* gravy browning
	A few drops of almond extract

Grease 1 large or 2 small molds; peel, core, and chop the apple; prepare the dried fruit.

Sift together the plain flour, self-rising flour, and salt into a mixing bowl. Add the bread crumbs, dried fruit, sugar, suet, candied peel, and grated lemon rind. Beat the eggs and milk together and stir them into the dry ingredients with the lemon

juice, adding more milk to make the mixture of a soft dropping consistency. Add a little caramel *or* gravy browning to slightly darken the mixture (about a level tsp.), and the almond extract. Mix in well. Turn into the mold, cover, and boil for 4 hr.

12 servings

CUMBERLAND PUDDING

1 cup peeled, cored, and coarsely chopped apple	1 cup currants
	⅜ cup brown sugar
2 cups flour	A little grated nutmeg
Pinch of salt	2 eggs
1 rounded tsp. baking powder	¼ cup milk (approx.)
½ cup finely chopped *or* shredded suet	

Grease a 1-qt. pudding mold. Mix the apples with the sifted flour, salt, and baking powder. Add the suet, currants, sugar, and nutmeg. Beat the eggs well and stir them into the mixture, adding milk to make a soft dropping consistency. Turn into the mold. Cover securely with greased paper and steam 2½ hr.

6 servings

APRICOT PUDDING (Baked)

1 pt. milk	1 12-oz. can apricots
1 pt. fresh bread crumbs *or* cake crumbs	¼ cup sugar
	2 eggs
Shortcrust pastry using 1¼-1½ cups flour, etc.	½ cup sherry
	¼-½ cup sugar for the meringue

Boil the milk, pour it over the bread crumbs and let them soak for ½ hr. Line the sides of a 9-in. pie dish with the pastry.

Strain the apricots, pass them through a fine sieve, and add ¼ cup sugar, egg yolks, sherry, and soaked crumbs to them. Pour into the pie dish. Bake in a fairly hot oven (200 °C, 400 °F) until the pastry is cooked and the filling is set — 25-30 min. Beat the egg whites until stiff, stir in the ¼-½ cup sugar, and spread this meringue over the top of the pudding. Dredge well with sugar and decorate with strips of angelica and cut glacé cherry, if liked. Bake in a very cool oven (150 °C, 290 °F) until the meringue is crisp and golden, about 30 min.

6 servings

COCONUT PUDDING

Shortcrust pastry using 1¼-1½ cups flour, etc.	3 eggs 1 cup cake crumbs
2 cups coconut	⅝ cup cream *or*
1 pt. milk	milk
3 tbs. butter	Vanilla extract
3 tbs. sugar	¼ cup sugar

Line the sides of a 9-in. pie dish with the pastry. Simmer the coconut in the 1 pt. milk until tender — about 10-15 min.; allow to cool. Cream together the butter and the 3 tbs. sugar until soft, work in the egg yolks one at a time, and add the cake crumbs, cream *or* milk, prepared coconut, and the vanilla extract. Pour the mixture into the pie dish and bake in a fairly hot oven (190 °C, 375 °F) until the pastry is cooked and the mixture set — about ½ hr. Stiffly beat the egg whites and fold in the ¼ cup sugar; pile on top of the pudding. Reduce oven heat to very cool (145 °C, 290 °F) and put the pudding back into oven until the meringue is golden — 30-40 min.

6 servings

ORANGE PUDDING

Shortcrust pastry using 1¼-1½ cups flour, etc.	2 cups cake crumbs *or* sponge cakes
4 oranges	Pinch of grated
1¼ cups milk	nutmeg
⅜ cup sugar	2 eggs

Line the sides of a 9-in. pie dish with the pastry. Thinly cut the rind from 1 orange and infuse this in the milk for about 20 min., then remove it. To the milk add the sugar, cake crumbs, nutmeg, well-beaten eggs, and lastly the juice of all the oranges. Pour into the lined pie dish and bake in a fairly hot oven (190 °C, 375 °F) until the pastry is cooked and the mixture is set — about 30-35 min.

WEST RIDING PUDDING

Shortcrust pastry using 1¼-1½ cups flour, etc.	2 eggs 1½ cups flour 1 tsp. baking
½ cup butter *or* margarine	powder Milk to mix
½ cup sugar	2 tbs. jam

Line and decorate the sides of a 9-in. pie dish with the pastry.

Cream the fat and sugar together until white and creamy. Beat in the eggs gradually. Beat thoroughly. Sift in the flour and baking powder. Stir in lightly, adding milk until the mixture drops easily from the spoon. Cover the bottom of the pie dish with jam, then spread on the mixture. Bake in a fairly hot oven (190 °C, 375 °F) for about 1 hr., until the pudding is cooked and nicely browned.

APPLE PUDDING (Steamed)

½ cup apples (after peeling and coring)	½ cup sugar Pinch of nutmeg Pinch of salt
2½ cups bread crumbs	2 eggs ⅝ cup milk
½ cup finely chopped suet	

Chop the apples. Mix together the bread crumbs, suet, sugar, nutmeg, and salt. Add the apples. Beat the eggs. Stir in the eggs and milk, and mix well. Let stand for 1 hr. to allow the bread to soak. The mixture should then drop easily from the spoon. If it is too stiff, add a little more milk. Pour into a well-greased bowl or mold, cover, and steam for 2 hr. Serve with Custard Sauce.

APRICOT PUDDING (Steamed)

6 pieces canned apricots	2 eggs Rind of ½ lemon
6 tbs. butter *or* margarine	¾ cup flour ¼ tsp. baking
⅜ cup sugar	powder

Grease a 1-qt. bowl or mold. Drain the apricots well and cut them into small pieces.

Cream together the fat and sugar and when really soft beat in the eggs gradually. Stir in the grated lemon rind, apricots, sifted flour, and baking powder. Turn the mixture into the mold, cover, and steam steadily 1¼-1½ hr. Serve with Apricot Sauce.

4 servings

BACHELOR'S PUDDING

⅔ cup dried fruit	1¼ cups bread
1½ cups flour	crumbs
Pinch of salt	⅜ cup suet
1 tsp. baking	1 egg
powder	Milk to mix
⅜ cup sugar	

Grease a pudding mold.
Clean the fruit. Mix together the sifted flour, salt, baking powder, sugar, bread crumbs, and suet. Stir in the dried fruit. Add the well-beaten egg and some of the milk. Stir, adding more milk as required, until the mixture drops easily from the spoon. Turn the mixture into the mold; cover with greased paper; steam for 2-2½ hr. When ready, dredge well with sugar.

4-5 servings

FINGER PUDDING

3 eggs	Pinch of ground
½ cup sugar	cloves
¾ cup ground	¼ cup melted
almonds	butter *or*
½ tsp. grated	margarine
lemon rind	½ cup crushed
¼ tsp. ground	ladyfingers
cinnamon	

Grease a mold.
Separate the eggs. Beat the yolks and sugar together until light and creamy. Add the ground almonds, lemon rind, cinnamon, cloves, melted fat, and crushed ladyfingers. Mix well. Stiffly beat the egg whites and fold them in. Pour the mixture into a well-greased mold. Steam gently for 1-1¼ hr.

5-6 servings

DATE ROLY-POLY PUDDING

1 cup dates	¼ tsp. salt
3 cups flour	½-¾ cup finely
2 rounded tsp.	chopped suet
baking powder	Water to mix

Chop the dates. Sift together the flour, baking powder, and salt. Add the suet and dates. Add sufficient water to mix to a soft but firm dough. Form into a roll and place at the end of a well-floured pudding cloth. Roll up loosely and tie firmly at either end, into a sausage shape. Drop into boiling water and simmer 2-2½ hr. Serve with custard.

Note: For dates the same weight of the following may be substituted — **currants, raisins,** or **figs,** and the pudding named accordingly.

DUCHESS PUDDING

2 tbs. pistachio nuts	3 eggs
1 cup macaroons	4 tbs. orange
6 tbs. butter *or*	marmalade
margarine	2 tsp. ground
⅜ cup sugar	rice

Grease a 1-qt. bowl or pudding mold. Blanch, peel, and chop the pistachios; sprinkle ½ around the sides and bottom of the mold. Crush the macaroons.
Cream together the fat and sugar. Separate the eggs. Work in the egg yolks and marmalade. Stir in the macaroons. Stiffly beat the egg whites and fold them in lightly. Sprinkle in the ground rice and the rest of the pistachios at the same time. Put the mixture into the mold; cover. Steam slowly for 1¼-1½ hr. Serve with Marmalade Sauce.

5-6 servings

FRUIT PUDDING WITH SUET CRUST

1½ lb. fresh fruit	¼-⅜ cup
as below	granulated
Suet-crust pastry	sugar

Prepare the fruit and mix it with the sugar. Sift the flour and baking powder; add the suet and salt. Mix with enough water to make a soft but firm dough. Grease and

35

line a bowl or mold *(see below)*. Fill to the top with the fruit and sugar and add 2½ tbs. cold water. Put on the top crust.

To boil: Cover with a well-floured cloth and boil for 2½-3 hr.

To steam: Cover with greased paper and steam for 2½-3 hr.

6 servings

Note: *To line a bowl* — cut off ¼ of the pastry for the top. Roll the remaining pastry ½ in. larger than the top of the bowl, drop the pastry into the greased bowl, and with the fingers work the pastry evenly up the sides to the top. Roll out the lid to the size of the top of the bowl, wet the edges, and secure it firmly around the inside of the pastry lining the bowl.

Suggested fillings:

Apples	Damsons
Blackberries and apples	Blueberries
	Plums
Black currants	Rhubarb
Cranberries	Peaches

GINGER PUDDING

2 cups flour	½ cup finely
1 tsp. ground	chopped suet
ginger	⅜ cup sugar
Pinch of salt	1 tbs. molasses
1 tsp. soda	1 egg
	Milk to mix

Grease a 5-cup bowl or mold. Prepare the suet.

Sift the flour, ginger, salt, and soda into a bowl. Add the finely chopped suet and sugar. Stir in the molasses, beaten egg, and sufficient milk to make a soft dropping consistency. Put the mixture into the bowl; cover. Steam for 2 hr. Turn out and serve with syrup sauce.

6 servings

GOLDEN OR MARMALADE PUDDING

½ cup marmalade	1 rounded tsp.
1 cup flour	baking powder
2½ cups bread crumbs	Pinch of salt
	2 eggs

⅜ cup finely chopped suet	⅝ cup milk (approx.)
¼ cup sugar	

Grease a 5-cup pudding mold. Put ¼ cup marmalade at the base.

Mix together the flour, bread crumbs, suet, sugar, baking powder, and salt. Beat together the eggs, remaining ¼ cup marmalade, and a little of the milk. Stir this into the dry ingredients and, using milk as required, mix to a very soft dropping consistency. Put the mixture into the mold and cover with greased paper. Steam for 1½-2 hr. Serve with Marmalade Sauce.

6 servings

ITALIAN PUDDING

⅝ cup cake crumbs	1½ tbs. raisins
⅝ cup bread crumbs	2 tbs. pistachio nuts, shredded
6 macaroons, pounded	1 tbs. rum *or* brandy
3 tbs. finely chopped candied peel	2 eggs

Put the cake crumbs, bread crumbs, macaroons, peel, raisins, and pistachios into a bowl. Beat together the brandy and eggs and stir into the mixture. Turn into a well-greased mold. Steam gently 1-1¼ hr. Serve with Custard Sauce.

3 servings

LEMON PUDDING

1½ cups flour	¼ cup sugar
Pinch of salt	Juice and rind of
1 rounded tsp. baking powder	1 lemon
4 tbs. butter *or* margarine	1 egg
	Milk to mix

Grease a 1-qt. pudding mold. Sift together the flour, salt, and baking powder. Rub in the fat and add the sugar and grated lemon rind. Mix to a soft dropping consistency with the beaten egg, lemon juice, and milk. Put the pudding into the greased mold and cover with greased paper. Steam for 1½-2 hr.

4-6 servings

NEWCASTLE PUDDING

3 tbs. glacé cherries	1½ cups flour
½ cup butter *or* margarine	Pinch of salt
½ cup sugar	1 tsp. baking powder
2 eggs	A little milk

Grease a 1-qt. mold or bowl and decorate with the cherries.

Cream the butter and sugar. Gradually beat in the eggs. Sift in the flour, salt, and baking powder, and mix with a little milk to a soft dropping consistency. Put the mixture into the bowl *or* mold; cover. Steam for 1½-2 hr. Turn out and serve with Jam Sauce.

6 servings

PRINCE ALBERT PUDDING

2½ cups prunes	½ cup sugar
2½ cups water	2 eggs
A few strips of lemon rind	Rind of ½ lemon
2 tbs. brown sugar	⅜ cup rice flour
½ cup butter *or* margarine	2½ cups brown bread crumbs

Prune Sauce:

1 tsp. arrowroot	Juice of ½ lemon
1¼ cups prune juice	Red food coloring
1 tbs. granulated sugar	

Wash and soak the prunes in the water overnight. Stew them with the strips of lemon rind and brown sugar until soft. Strain them (reserving the liquid for the sauce) and remove the stones.

Completely line a dry mold or bowl with the prunes, as follows: halve each prune; dip in clarified butter *or* margarine; press skin-side against the mold. Chop any prunes left over.

Cream the butter and sugar together. Separate the eggs; beat in the yolks. Add the grated lemon rind, chopped prunes, rice flour, and brown bread crumbs. Fold in the stiffly-beaten egg whites. Turn mix-

ture into the mold; cover. Steam gently for 1¾ hr.

Meanwhile make the sauce: blend the arrowroot with some of the prune juice. Boil the remainder of the syrup and pour it over the blended arrowroot; return to pan and simmer for 3 min. Add the sugar and juice of ½ lemon; color pink with a few drops of red food coloring.

Turn out the pudding and coat with the sauce.

6 servings

ROLY-POLY PUDDING

3 cups flour	Pinch of salt
2 rounded tsp. baking powder	Water to mix Jam
¾ cup finely chopped suet	

Sift the flour and baking powder; add the suet and salt. Mix with sufficient water to make a soft but firm dough. Roll it into a rectangle about ¼ in. thick. Spread with jam almost to the edge. Dampen the edges and roll up lightly. Seal the edges. Wrap the pudding in a scalded well-floured cloth; tie up the ends. Put into fast boiling water. Simmer for 2-2½ hr.

5 servings

SPICED RHUBARB PUDDING

3¾ cups rhubarb	1 tsp. ground cinnamon
⅜ cup currants	
¾ cup raisins	Suet-crust pastry using 2 cups flour
¼ cup brown sugar	
1 tsp. mixed spices	

Grease a 5-cup bowl. Wipe and cut the rhubarb into pieces about ½ in. long and mix with the dried fruit, sugar, and spices.

Make the suet-crust pastry. Divide the crust into 3 portions varying in size. Put the smallest portion at the bottom of the bowl; cover it with ½ of the rhubarb mixture. Roll out the second piece of crust and put it on top. Add the rest of the rhubarb mixture; cover with the third piece of rolled-out crust. Cover with waxed paper. Steam for 2-2½ hr.

6 servings

SPOTTED PUDDING

3 cups flour	¾ cup finely
2 rounded tsp.	chopped suet
baking powder	½ cup sugar
Pinch of salt	1 cup currants
	Milk to mix

Sift together the flour, baking powder and salt. Add the suet, sugar, and fruit and mix with the milk to a soft dough. Form into a roll and turn onto a well-floured cloth. Roll up the cloth loosely, and tie at both ends, leaving enough room for the pudding to swell. Drop into boiling water and simmer for 2 hr.; *or* steam for 2½ hr. Serve with Custard *or* Lemon Sauce.

6 servings

SUET PUDDING (Plain, for Sweet or Savory Dishes)

3 cups flour	½-¾ cup finely
¼ tsp. salt	chopped suet
2 rounded tsp.	Water to mix
baking powder	

Sift the flour, salt, and baking powder. Mix in the suet. Add cold water, stirring gradually until a stiff dough is formed. Shape the dough into a roll. Put the dough into a scalded, well-floured pudding cloth and roll up loosely. Tie the ends securely with string. Put into a saucepan of boiling water and boil gently for 1½-2 hr., adding more boiling water, if necessary, to keep the pudding covered. Serve plain with meat or with jam, honey, Fruit, or Marmalade Sauce.

6-7 servings

RAISIN PUDDING

½ cup butter *or*	½ cup sugar
margarine	¾ cup raisins
2 cups flour	2 eggs
Pinch of salt	Milk to mix
1 heaping tsp.	A few drops
baking powder	vanilla extract

Grease a 5-cup bowl. Clean the raisins. Rub the fat into the sifted flour, salt, and baking powder. Add the sugar and fruit. Mix with beaten egg, milk, and vanilla extract to a soft dropping consistency. Put

the mixture into the bowl; cover. Steam for 1½-2 hr. Turn out, dredge with sugar, and serve with Custard or Lemon Sauce.

6 servings

SYRUP SPONGE PUDDING

1½ cups flour	1 tsp. soda
3¾ cups bread	Pinch of salt
crumbs	1 egg
½ cup finely	2 tbs. light
chopped suet	corn syrup
¼ cup sugar	1 tbs. molasses
1 tsp. ground	Milk to mix
ginger	

Grease a bowl and, if liked, put an extra tbs. of corn syrup in the bottom. Mix together the flour, bread crumbs, suet, sugar, ginger, soda, and salt. Beat the egg with the corn syrup, molasses, and a little of the milk. Stir this into the other ingredients, using more milk if required, to mix to a very soft dropping consistency. Put the mixture into the bowl; cover with greased paper. Steam for 1½-2 hr.

6-7 servings

TRANSPARENT PUDDINGS

6 tbs. butter *or*	3 eggs
margarine	2 tbs. apricot
⅜ cup sugar	jam

Butter well 6 dariole molds.

Cream together the fat and sugar until lighter in color and quite soft. Add each egg separately and beat well. One-third fill each mold with this mixture and put 2 tsp. of apricot jam on top; then cover with the remaining mixture, so that the molds are about ¾ full. Cover with greased paper. Steam slowly for about 25 min. Let the puddings cool slightly before turning them out, to lessen the risk of their breaking. Serve at once with custard.

6 servings

MOLASSES PUDDING

1¼ cups bread	½ lb. molasses *or*
crumbs	corn syrup
Rind of 1 lemon	(approx.)
Suet-crust pastry	

Sift flour, salt, and baking powder, and mix with suet and sufficient water to make a soft but firm dough. Divide the dough into 2 equal portions, using 1 portion to line a 5-cup bowl. Cut enough from the other portion to make the lid; roll out the remainder thinly.

Mix the bread crumbs and grated lemon rind. Put a layer of molasses in the bowl; sprinkle well with the bread crumbs. Cover with a round of the thinly rolled pastry. Moisten the edge of it with water and join securely to the pastry at the side of the bowl. Add another layer of molasses, crumbs, and pastry; then more molasses and crumbs. Finally, cover with the rolled-out top as the last layer of pastry. Cover with greased paper. Steam for 2½ hr.

6-7 servings

WELLINGTON PUDDING

2 tbs. granulated sugar for the caramel	½ tsp. ground nutmeg
2½ cups brown bread crumbs	¾ cup raisins
1 cup flour	3 tbs. finely chopped candied orange peel
Pinch of salt	
1 tsp. baking powder	½ cup sugar
½ cup finely chopped suet	3 eggs
½ tsp. ground cinnamon	⅝ cup milk (approx.)
	½ cup Marsala *or* sherry (optional)

Puree:

1 lb. chestnuts	A few drops of vanilla extract
Pinch of salt	
A little milk	Sugar to sweeten
2 tbs. cream	

Grease a 5-cup mold with butter.

Make the caramel by heating the granulated sugar with a little water until dissolved, then boil rapidly until the syrup is golden brown. Then quickly throw in, all at once, 3 tbs. of cold water; lower the heat and let the caramel dissolve.

Mix together the bread crumbs, sifted flour, salt, baking powder, suet, cinnamon, nutmeg, raisins, peel, and sugar. Beat together the eggs, the cooled caramel, and a little of the milk. Stir this into the dry ingredients, adding the wine (if used) and using more milk, if necessary, to mix to a soft dropping consistency. Pour into a well-buttered mold — only ¾ fill it. Cover with greased paper. Steam for 2½-2¾ hr.

Prepare the Chestnut Puree by cooking the chestnuts for 10 min. in boiling water with a pinch of salt, then skinning them. Put the chestnuts with a little milk in a saucepan; cook until tender. Rub them through a fine sieve; add the cream and vanilla; sweeten to taste.

Turn the mold onto a hot dish. Pipe the puree quickly into the center. Serve with Apricot Sauce poured around.

6 servings

BAKED PUDDINGS, GENERAL HINTS

1) Butter the dish, pan, or mold well, so that the pudding is easily turned out or served.
2) Wipe around the edges of the pie dish before baking.
3) The pudding is easier to handle if it is placed on a baking sheet while cooking.
4) Oven settings may vary with different cookers, so average settings in the recipes are given for general guidance.

ALMOND CASTLES

6 tbs. butter	1 tbs. brandy (optional)
⅜ cup sugar	
3 eggs	1 cup ground almonds
3 tbs. cream *or* milk	

Grease 8 dariole molds.

Cream together the butter and sugar. Stir in the egg yolks, cream or milk, brandy (if used), and almonds. Beat the egg whites to a stiff froth and add lightly to the rest of the ingredients. Three-quarters fill the molds. Bake in a warm oven (175 °C, 335 °F) 20-25 min., until the puddings are firm in the center and golden brown. Turn out and serve with custard.

6-7 servings

Apple Charlotte

APPLE CHARLOTTE

6 medium cooking apples	8 thinly cut slices of bread and butter
½ cup brown sugar	Sugar
Grated rind and juice of 1 lemon	

Grease a 5-cup charlotte mold with butter. Peel, core, and slice the apples. Place a layer in the bottom of the mold and sprinkle with sugar, grated lemon rind, and lemon juice. Cover with thin slices of bread and butter. Repeat until the dish is full, finishing with a layer of bread and butter. Cover with greased paper. Bake in a moderate oven (180 °C, 350 °F) for ¾-1 hr. Turn out of the dish, if desired, and dredge well with sugar before serving.

Alternatively, cut the bread ¼-in. thick before buttering it; line the mold with it, buttered side out, so that the pieces fit tightly together. Fill with the remaining ingredients packed tightly, and bake as above.

5-6 servings

APPLE OR OTHER FRUIT CRUMBLE

4-5 medium apples	6 tbs. butter *or* margarine
½ cup brown sugar	1½ cups flour
A little grated lemon rind	⅜ cup sugar
¼ cup water (approx.)	¼ tsp. ground ginger

Peel, core, and slice the apples into a pan.

40

Add ¼ cup water, ½ cup brown sugar, and lemon rind. With lid on the pan, cook gently until soft. Place in a greased 9-in. pie dish. Rub the fat into the flour until of the consistency of fine bread crumbs. Add the sugar and ground ginger, and mix well. Sprinkle the crumble over the apple; press down lightly. Bake in a moderate oven (180 °C, 350 °F) until the crumble is golden brown and the apples are fully cooked; this takes 30-40 min., depending on the cooking quality of the apples. Dredge with sugar and serve with custard *or* cream.

The same weight of the following may be substituted for apples: damsons, blueberries, peaches, pears, plums, raspberries, *or* rhubarb, and the crumble named accordingly.

6 servings

APPLE SNOW

6 medium	2 eggs
cooking apples	1¼ cups milk
Lemon rind	1 tbs. sugar
½ cup sugar	¼ cup sugar
1 tbs. cream	
(optional)	

Peel, core, and slice the apples. Stew with the lemon rind in ¼ cup water until tender. Put through a fine nylon sieve. Add ½ cup sugar and the cream, if used. In another bowl separate the eggs. Heat the milk and pour onto the well-beaten yolks; return to the pan and heat gently until the mixture thickens. Add 1 tbs. sugar. Put the apple puree into a buttered pie dish; pour the custard on top. Put into a warm oven (175 °C, 335 °F) until set — about 40 min. Stiffly beat the egg whites; stir in the ¼ cup sugar. Pile on top of the mixture. Bake in a very cool oven (145 °C, 290 °F) until meringue is slightly colored.

6 servings

BAKED APPLES

6 cooking apples	¼ cup water
¼ cup brown	
sugar	

Filling, choice of:

1) ¼ cup brown	1½ cups stoned
sugar; 4 tbs.	dates, currants, *or*
butter	raisins; ¼ cup
2) Black currant,	sugar; 1 tsp.
raspberry,	ground
strawberry, *or*	cinnamon
apricot jam	

Prepare the filling. Wash and core the apples. Cut around the skin of the apple with the tip of a sharp knife, ⅔ of the way up from the base. Put the apples into a baking dish and fill the centers with the chosen filling. Sprinkle with the brown sugar. Add the water. Bake in a moderate oven (180 °C, 350 °F) until the apples are soft in the center — about ¾-1 hr., depending on the cooking quality of the apples.

6 servings

BAKED JAM ROLL

3 cups flour	¾ cup finely
1 tsp. baking	chopped suet
powder	Jam
Pinch of salt	

Mix the flour, baking powder, salt, and suet with sufficient water to make a soft but firm dough. Roll the dough into a rectangle about ¼ in. thick. Spread with jam almost to the edges, dampen the edges, and roll up lightly. Seal the edges. Put onto a well-greased baking sheet. Cook in a fairly hot oven (200 °C, 400 °F) until cooked through, about 1 hr.

6 servings

BROWN BETTY

3¾ cups bread	4 tbs. light
crumbs	corn syrup
6 medium	½ cup brown
tart apples	sugar
1 lemon	
2 tbs. water	

Grease a 9-in. pie dish. Coat it with a layer of bread crumbs. Peel, core, and thinly slice the apples. Fill the pie dish with alternate layers of apples, grated lemon rind, and bread crumbs. Heat the syrup, sugar, and water in a pan, add the lemon juice, and pour this over the mixture. Bake in a warm oven (175 °C, 335 °F) 1¼-1½ hr., until the pudding is brown and the apple cooked.

6 servings

CHERRY PUDDING

3 cups cooking cherries	⅝ cup cream *or* milk
¼ cup water	Pinch of salt
⅝ cup sugar	3 eggs
¾ cup flour	Grated rind of ½ lemon
2-3 tbs. milk (approx.)	Pinch of ground cinnamon

Stone the cherries and stew them very gently (to keep them whole) in a small saucepan with the water and ⅜ cup sugar. Allow to cool. Blend the flour with the 2-3 tbs. of milk, so that it is smooth and "runny." Boil the cream *or* milk and add the blended flour to it, beating well to keep the mixture smooth. Bring to a boil again and add the ¼ cup sugar and salt. Cool the mixture. Separate the eggs. Beat the egg yolks into the mixture. Add the lemon rind, cinnamon, and lastly the stiffly beaten egg whites. Put into a well-greased mold or pie dish a layer of cherries and a layer of mixture alternately until the mold is full. Cover with greased paper. Bake in a fairly hot oven (200 °C, 400 °F) for about 40 min. Serve with a sweet sauce or fruit syrup.

5-6 servings

CHESTNUT PUDDING

6 oz. chestnuts, weighed after the skins have been removed	½ cup flour 1¼ cups cake crumbs
Pinch of salt	3 eggs
1 oz. plain chocolate	4 tbs. butter *or* margarine
1¼ cups milk	½ tsp. vanilla extract
	2 tbs. sugar

Wash the chestnuts, make a slit in each, and boil in water for about 10 min. Remove both skins and put the chestnuts into a saucepan with a very little water and the salt. Cook until tender, strain, dry,

and rub through a fine sieve.

Grate the chocolate, put it in the milk, and simmer until dissolved. Allow to cool slightly.

In another pan melt the butter; stir in the flour; cook for 2-3 min. Work in the milk and chocolate gradually, keeping the mixture smooth; stir until it boils. Add the cake crumbs and continue cooking until the mixture leaves the sides of the pan. Allow to cool. Separate the eggs. Beat the egg yolks, chestnut puree, vanilla extract, and sugar into the mixture. Beat the egg whites to a stiff froth and fold them lightly into the mixture. Pour into a well-buttered mold. Cover with buttered paper. Bake in a fairly hot oven (190 °C, 375 °F) for 1 hr., *or* steam for 1½ hr. Serve with Custard Sauce.

6-7 servings

CHOCOLATE PUDDING

1½ cups flour	½ cup sugar
Pinch of salt	¼ cup cocoa
1 rounded tsp. baking powder	1 egg Milk to mix
6 tbs. butter *or* margarine	A few drops of vanilla extract

Sift together the flour, salt, and baking powder. Rub in the fat. Add the sugar and cocoa; mix well. Add the beaten egg and milk and mix to a dropping consistency. Add the vanilla extract. Put into a greased pan or pie dish. Bake in a fairly hot oven (190 °C, 375 °F) for 30-40 min. Dredge well with sugar and serve with Chocolate *or* Custard Sauce.

6 servings

EVE'S PUDDING

3 medium apples	½ cup sugar
2 tbs. water	2 eggs
¼-½ cup granulated *or* brown sugar	Grated rind of ½ lemon
4 cloves (optional)	½ cup flour
½ cup butter *or* margarine	1 tsp. baking powder

Peel, core, and thinly slice the apples. Put them into a small saucepan with the water, granulated *or* brown sugar, and cloves if used. Cook very slowly (with the lid on the pan) until the apples are soft, stirring occasionally to prevent them from burning. Remove the cloves. Put the apples into the bottom of a well-greased pie dish.

Cream together the fat and ½ cup sugar. Beat in the eggs gradually. Add the grated lemon rind. Sift in the flour and baking powder. Mix to a soft dropping consistency. Spread this mixture over the apples. Bake in a moderate oven (180 °C, 350 °F) for 40-45 min.

4 servings

FRIAR'S OMELET

2½ cups bread crumbs	½ cup granulated sugar
6 medium cooking apples	1 lemon
4 tbs. butter *or* margarine	2 eggs

Grease a 9-in. pie dish and put ½ the bread crumbs into it. Core, peel, and slice the apples. Stew them with the fat, sugar, grated rind and juice of lemon, and a tbs. of water, until tender. Cool slightly. Beat the eggs well and add them to the mixture. Pour the apple mixture into the pie dish. Cover with the rest of the bread crumbs. Flake a few pieces of butter on top. Bake in a hot oven (220 °C, 425 °F) for 20 min.

4-5 servings

FRUIT PUDDING

2½ cups sweetened, stewed fresh fruit	6 tbs. butter
	⅜ cup sugar
2 cups flour	2 eggs
1 tsp. baking powder	Pinch of salt
	Mix to mix

Grease a pie dish. Strain the syrup from the fruit and lay the fruit at the bottom of the pie dish. The syrup can be used for making a sauce to serve with the pudding. (Leftover stewed fruit can be used for this purpose; it is not essential to have the exact amount, but there should be enough fruit to cover the pie dish to a depth of at least ½ in.).

Sift together the flour, baking powder, and salt, and rub in the fat. Add the sugar. Mix to a dropping consistency with the beaten eggs and milk. Spread this mixture over the fruit. Bake in a fairly hot oven (190 °C, 375 °F) for 40-45 min., until the pudding mixture is cooked through and brown on top. Dredge well with sugar. Serve with Fruit *or* Custard Sauce *or* thin cream.

Note: If raw fruit is used, prepare it in the usual way. Stew it in as little water as possible, sweeten to taste, and let it cool before putting the pudding mixture on top.

6 servings

LEMON PUDDING

4 tbs. butter *or* margarine	Rind and juice of 1½ lemons
½ cup sugar	1½ cups flour
3 eggs	1¼ cups milk

Grease a 9-in. pie dish.

Cream together the butter and sugar until soft. Beat in the egg yolks. Add the grated lemon rind and the sifted flour. Stir in the milk and lemon juice. Fold in the stiffly beaten egg whites. Pour the mixture into the buttered pie dish. Bake in a moderate oven (180 °C, 350 °F) for 45 min., until firm and brown.

4 servings

Pear Crumble

Sauces

APPLE SAUCE

3 medium apples	Rind and juice of ½ lemon
2 tbs. water	Sugar to taste
1 tbs. butter *or* margarine	

Stew the apples very gently with the water, butter, and lemon rind until they are pulpy. Beat them until smooth, or rub them through a hair or nylon sieve. Reheat the sauce with the lemon juice and sweeten to taste. Serve with Ginger Pudding.

APRICOT SAUCE

4-6 apricots, fresh *or* canned	Lemon juice
⅝ cup water *or* syrup from can	1 tsp. maraschino (optional)
2-4 tbs. brown sugar	1 tsp. arrowroot

Stone the apricots and stew them in the water until soft. Then rub them through a hair or nylon sieve. Meanwhile crack the stones; scald and skin the kernels. Add sugar, lemon juice, liqueur (if used), and kernels to the sauce. Reheat the sauce, stirring in the arrowroot blended with a little cold water. Bring to a boil and serve the sauce.

Today a sauce of sieved, warmed apricot jam with a little lemon juice added is more usually served.

ARROWROOT SAUCE

1 rounded tsp. arrowroot	Lemon rind
	Sugar
1¼ cups fruit juice *or* white wine and fruit juice *or* cider	Lemon juice

Blend the arrowroot with a little cold liquid. Boil the rest of the liquid with lemon juice and rind to taste. Remove rind and stir the boiling liquid into the blended arrowroot, return the mixture to the pan, and bring it just to boiling point. Sweeten to taste.

BRANDY BUTTER (Hard Sauce)

6 tbs. butter	1 tsp.-1 tbs. brandy
1½ cups confectioners' sugar *or* 1 cup confectioners' sugar and 3 tbs. ground almonds	1 whipped egg white (optional)

Cream the butter until soft. Sift the confectioners' sugar, and cream it with the butter until white and light in texture. Mix in the almonds, if used. Work the brandy carefully into the mixture. Fold the stiffly beaten egg white into the sauce. Serve with Christmas or other steamed puddings.

Note: This sauce may be stored for several weeks in an airtight jar. It makes an excellent filling for sweet sandwiches.

BRANDY SAUCE (ECONOMICAL)

1 tsp. arrowroot *or* cornstarch	1 egg yolk
⁵⁄₈ cup milk	5 tbs. good brandy
	1 tsp. sugar

Blend the arrowroot with a little cold milk. Heat the rest of the milk and, when boiling, stir it into the blended arrowroot. Return mixture to pan and bring to boiling point. Mix together the egg yolk, brandy, and sugar. Cool the arrowroot sauce a little, then stir the egg mixture into it. Cook without boiling until the egg yolk thickens.

BRANDY SAUCE (RICH)

⁵⁄₈ cup light cream	2 tsp. sugar
2 egg yolks	5 tbs. good brandy

Mix all ingredients in a bowl. Set the bowl over a saucepan of boiling water and beat steadily until the mixture thickens.

BUTTERSCOTCH SAUCE

½ cup dark brown sugar	1 tsp. arrowroot
⁵⁄₈ cup water	A few drops of vanilla extract
2 tbs. butter	A few drops of lemon juice
1 strip of lemon rind	

Dissolve the sugar in the ⁵⁄₈ cup water, add the butter and lemon rind and boil for 5 min. Remove lemon rind. Blend the arrowroot with 2 tsp. water; thicken the sauce with the blended arrowroot. Add vanilla and lemon juice to taste.

CARAMEL SAUCE

¼ cup sugar *or* light corn syrup	1¼ cups custard sauce
5 tbs. water	Lemon juice *or* vanilla extract

Put the sugar and 2 tbs. water in a small pan; dissolve the sugar over gentle heat; then boil the syrup until it is a deep golden brown. Add the rest of the water to the caramel and leave it in a warm place to dissolve. If golden syrup is used, heat it without water until of a golden-brown color, then dissolve it in the water. Add the dissolved caramel to the custard sauce, and flavor to taste.

CHANTILLY APPLE SAUCE

3 medium cooking apples	2 tbs. butter
3 tbs. sugar	⁵⁄₈ cup cream

Peel, core, and slice the apples; put them in a saucepan with 2-3 tbs. cold water. Add the butter and sugar, cook gently until tender, then rub through a nylon sieve. Whip the cream until stiff; stir it into the apple puree; use as required.

CHERRY SAUCE

1½ cups freshly stewed *or* bottled cherries	2 tbs. red currant jelly
⁵⁄₈ cup juice in which cherries were cooked *or* bottled	Pepper
	1-2 tsp. vinegar
	2 tbs. red wine
Sugar to taste	½ tsp. arrowroot (optional)

Stone the cherries. Heat all ingredients together and simmer the sauce until the juice is slightly syrupy, or blend the arrowroot with 1 tsp. cold water and add it to thicken the liquid.

CHOCOLATE RUM SAUCE

3 oz. dessert chocolate	1 tsp. vanilla extract
1 pt. stock syrup	2 egg yolks
	Rum to taste

Grate the chocolate into a metal bowl and set it over very hot water. Stir until melted. Add the syrup gradually, stirring continually until smooth. Then beat in the beaten egg yolks and the rum.

For the stock syrup

Boil 4 cups sugar in 2½ cups water to 220 °F, skimming if necessary while it boils. Remove from the heat, cool, and store.

CHOCOLATE SAUCE (PLAIN)

3 oz. bitter chocolate *or* cooking chocolate *or* 1 heaping tbs. cocoa	Sugar if required Vanilla extract 1 tsp. rum (optional) A few drops coffee flavoring (optional)
1¼ cups water 1 tbs. cornstarch	

Break the chocolate in pieces and warm them gently with a very little water. When melted, beat the chocolate mixture until smooth, adding the rest of the water gradually. Thicken the sauce with the cornstarch blended with a little cold water. Flavor and sweeten to taste.

If cocoa is used, mix it with the dry cornstarch before blending with water.

CHOCOLATE SAUCE (RICH)

4 oz. chocolate	1 tsp. rum
1¼ cups milk	Sugar, if required
2-3 egg yolks	1 egg white
Vanilla extract	(optional)

Dissolve the chocolate in the milk. Make a custard with the egg yolks and the chocolate-flavored milk — *see* Custard Sauce. Flavor and sweeten to taste. If liked, 1 egg white may be whipped to a stiff froth and folded into the finished sauce.

COFFEE SAUCE

⅝ cup very strong coffee	Sugar to taste Vanilla extract (optional)
⅝ cup milk	
1 heaping tsp. cornstarch	1 tsp. rum (optional)
1 egg yolk	

Thicken the coffee and milk with the cornstarch (*see* Cornstarch Sauce). Cool the sauce, add the egg yolk, and cook it without boiling. Sweeten and flavor to taste.

CORNSTARCH CUSTARD

2 tbs. cornstarch	Flavoring
1¼ cups milk	1 egg yolk
2 tsp. sugar	

Blend the cornstarch with a little of the cold milk. Boil the rest of the milk with thinly cut lemon rind if used for flavoring. Remove rind and stir the boiling liquid into the blended cornstarch. Rinse the pan and return the sauce to it. Boil for 3 min. Sweeten and flavor the sauce unless lemon rind has been used. Cool the sauce, add the egg yolk and sugar, and cook at low heat until the egg thickens without boiling. At once pour out of the pan into a bowl or sauce boat. Flavor, and add extra sweetening if required.

CORNSTARCH SAUCE

1¼ cups milk	Lemon rind *or* any flavor to blend with the flavor of pudding it accompanies
2 tbs. cornstarch	
2 tsp. sugar	

Blend the cornstarch with a little of the cold milk. Boil the rest of the milk with the thinly cut lemon rind if used. Remove rind and stir the boiling liquid into the blended cornstarch. Rinse the pan and return the sauce to it. Bring to boiling point and boil for 3 min. Sweeten and flavor the sauce, unless lemon rind has been used for flavoring.

CRANBERRY SAUCE

2 cups cranberries	Sugar to taste
⅝-1¼ cups water	

Stew the cranberries until soft, using ⅝ cup water and adding more if needed. Rub the fruit through a hair or nylon sieve. Sweeten to taste. For economy, half cranberries and half sour cooking apples make an excellent sauce.

CURRANT SAUCE

⅜ cup washed, dried currants	A little grated lemon rind
¼ cup flour	Juice of ½ lemon
2 tbs. butter *or* margarine	A pinch of powdered nutmeg
1¼ cups water	
Sugar to taste	A pinch of cloves
¼ cup red *or* white wine	A pinch of ginger

Fry the flour in the butter until golden brown. Stir in the water, bring the sauce to boiling point, add remaining ingredients, and simmer for 10 min.

CUSTARD SAUCE

2 tsp. sugar	1¼ cups milk
2 egg yolks *or* 1 whole egg	Flavoring

Mix together the sugar and egg yolks *or* whole egg. Warm the milk until about lukewarm preferably in the top of a double boiler. Stir the milk into the egg, return everything to the rinsed pan, and cook at low heat until the egg thickens, without boiling, or the egg will curdle. At once pour out of the pan into a bowl or sauce boat. Flavor, and add extra sweetening if required. If the custard should curdle, beat it vigorously just before serving.

FROTHY OR WHIPPED SHERRY SAUCE

⅝ cup milk	Flavoring of
1 tbs. sugar	lemon rind *or*
¼ cup sherry *or* white wine	any spice, if desired

Heat the milk. Dissolve the sugar in the milk; then allow to cool a little. Beat the eggs and sherry together; add the warm milk. In a bowl, placed over boiling water, beat all ingredients until the sauce is thick and frothy. Serve at once.

FRUIT SAUCE
Suitable fruits are: damsons, plums, raspberries, red currants, blackberries.

1 lb. fresh fruit	Lemon juice, if
A very little water to stew	liked
	1 tsp. (rounded)
Sugar to sweeten	arrowroot to each 1¼ cups puree

Stew the fruit in the water until soft; sieve it. Sweeten, flavor, and thicken the sauce with arrowroot blended with a little cold water or fruit juice.

FRUIT AND YOGURT SAUCE (COLD)

1¼ cups fruit purée	Sugar to sweeten
1¼ cups plain yogurt	

Carefully mix the cold fruit puree and yogurt together. Sweeten well.

GINGER SAUCE

1¼ cups cornstarch *or* Custard Sauce	Lemon juice
	½ tsp. grated
1 tsp. ground ginger	lemon rind (optional)
Golden syrup to sweeten	

Stir the ginger into the sauce, sweeten, and flavor with lemon juice and rind if liked.

Note: Caramel Sauce with the addition of ginger is also good.

GINGER SYRUP SAUCE

½ cup brown sugar	1 tsp. arrowroot
	½ tsp. ground
1¼ cups water *or* ⅝ cup syrup from preserved ginger and ⅝ cup water	ginger
	1 tsp. lemon juice
Piece of root ginger	1 tbs. chopped preserved ginger
Strip of lemon rind	

Dissolve the sugar in the water, add the root ginger and lemon rind, and simmer for 15 min. Blend the arrowroot and ground ginger with a little cold water and the lemon juice, and thicken the sauce with this. Add the preserved ginger and simmer the sauce for 2-3 min.

GOOSEBERRY SAUCE

2 cups green gooseberries	Salt and pepper
	1 tsp.
⅝ cup water	elderberries
1 tbs. butter	(optional)

2 tbs. sugar	A few chopped
Lemon juice	sorrel leaves
Nutmeg	(optional)

Stew the gooseberries at low heat with the water and butter until they are pulpy. Beat or blend them until smooth, or rub them through a hair or nylon sieve. Reheat the sauce; stir in the sugar; add lemon juice and grated nutmeg to taste; season. Stir in the berries and sorrel if used.

JAM SAUCE

4 good tbs. jam	1 heaping tsp.
1¼ cups water	arrowroot
Sugar	Coloring, if
Lemon juice	needed

Boil the jam and water together, add sugar and lemon juice to taste, and thicken with the arrowroot blended with a little cold water. Strain the sauce if the jam has seeds. Color if necessary.

LEMON SAUCE

Rind of ½ lemon	Juice of 2 lemons
1¼ cups water	1 heaping tsp.
½ cup sugar *or*	arrowroot
corn syrup to	
sweeten	

Steep the thinly cut lemon rind in the water for 15 min., then remove it. Add sugar or syrup to flavored water and boil for 5 min. Add the lemon juice and thicken the sauce with the arrowroot blended with a little cold water.

Note: If a richer sauce is desired, a small glass of sherry and an egg yolk can be added to the above a few min. before serving, but the sauce must not be allowed to boil again once the egg yolk has been added.

MARMALADE SAUCE (1)

As for Jam Sauce above, substituting marmalade for jam. Do not strain the sauce.

MARMALADE SAUCE (2)

| 4 tbs. stiff | ¼ cup white |
| marmalade | wine |

Heat the marmalade and wine together.

MOUSSELINE SAUCE

1 egg	¼ cup cream
1 egg yolk	1 tbs. sherry
3 tbs. sugar	*or* fruit juice

Separate the egg white from the yolk and whip it to a stiff froth. Put all other ingredients into a bowl placed over a pan of hot water and beat until creamy and thick. Fold the egg white into the hot sauce. Serve at once.

ORANGE SAUCE

Like Lemon Sauce, but use much less sugar. Beat over gentle heat or in a double boiler until the sauce thickens. It must not boil.

PRUNE SAUCE

1⅓ cups prunes	Pinch of ground
1¼ cups water	cinnamon
1 strip of lemon	1 tbs. rum *or*
rind	brandy
2 tbs. sugar	(optional)
	Lemon juice

Soak the prunes overnight in the water. Stew them with the lemon rind until quite soft. Rub them through a hair, nylon, or fine-wire sieve. Add the other ingredients to taste.

It is good with spicy hot puddings.

QUINCE SAUCE

½ lb. quinces	Sugar
1¼ cups water *or*	Ground clove
water in which	Lemon juice
carrots cooked	¼ cup red wine
Ground	(optional)
nutmeg	

Stew the quinces very gently in the water until pulpy. Beat them quite smooth or rub them through a hair or nylon sieve. Reheat the sauce, add nutmeg, sugar, clove, and lemon juice to taste. Stir in the red wine, if used.

RED CURRENT SAUCE

½ cup red currant jelly	¼ cup port or other red wine

Heat the two ingredients together at low heat until the jelly is melted.
Serve with game, venison or as a sweet sauce with puddings.

RICH SWEET SAUCE

4 egg yolks or 2 whole eggs ½ cup sugar ⅝ cup cream	⅝ cup milk Grated rind of 1 orange

Beat the egg yolks or whole eggs with the sugar and milk until well-mixed. Add the orange rind and cream, and cook over very low heat or in a double boiler until the sauce thickens. It must not boil.

RUM BUTTER

½ cup butter 1 cup brown sugar	¼ cup rum

Beat the butter to a cream and beat in the sugar. When light and creamy, gradually add the rum. Transfer to a serving dish and chill thoroughly before using.

SABAYON SAUCE (HOT or COLD)

2 egg yolks 2 tbs. sugar	⅝ cup Marsala wine or Madeira

In a saucepan beat the egg yolks and sugar until very light and frothy. Stir in the wine, and over very gentle heat continue

beating briskly until the sauce rises; it must not boil. Serve at once.

SHERRY BUTTER

As for Rum Butter, using sherry in place of rum and granulated sugar in place of brown sugar.

SWEET MELTED-BUTTER SAUCE

To 1¼ cups white sauce add 2 tbs. butter, sweeten to taste, and add any sweet flavoring desired.

RAISIN SAUCE

As for Currant Sauce, substituting raisins for currants.

WHIPPED EGG SAUCE

2 egg yolks 1 tbs. sugar	¼ cup sherry or fruit juice or water and suitable flavoring

Put all the ingredients in a china bowl; Beat them until well-mixed. Place the bowl over boiling water and continue beating until the sauce thickens. Serve at once.

WINE SAUCE

¼ cup water ¼ cup sherry 2 tbs. any jam or jelly	Sugar to taste Lemon juice to taste

Boil all ingredients together for 5 min. Rub through a hair or nylon sieve, or strain the sauce. Adjust the flavor; reheat if necessary. If liked, this sauce may be thickened as Jam Sauce.

Cold "Set" Milk and Gelatin Desserts

Like hot milk puddings cold "set" milk desserts can be light and bland or rich and creamy, varying from a simple, plain blancmange to a luxurious Riz à l'Impératrice. All, however, are first cooked just like hot milk puddings.

They can also be molded like jellies, if they contain enough eggs, or some gelatin to set them firmly.

Jellies can also be varied more than we sometimes think. For instance, they can be strained, clear and sparkling, or whipped to a foam. Here is a choice to give you some new ideas.

COLD MILKY DESSERTS, GENERAL HINTS

1) Simmer whole grains, such as rice, gently in milk until all the grains are soft and the milk has almost been absorbed. Use a double boiler or thick-bottomed pan, and stir the mixture occasionally while it cooks gently (1½-2 hr.).

Sprinkle small grain, such as semolina, dry into near-boiling milk, and stir continually while it cooks (10-15 min.).

Blend powdered grain such as cornstarch with a little cold milk. Heat the rest of the milk almost to boiling point, and pour it onto the grain, stirring constantly. Pour back into the pan, and simmer, stirring, until the grain is cooked (4-5 min.).

2) Add a pat of butter to any grain mixture; it improves its taste and texture.   .

3) All these mixtures are ready for molding when a spoonful dropped back onto the hot surface merges into it only if shaken gently. Cook a little longer if it is too slack; add a little milk if it is too stiff.

4) Use a china or glass mold, if possible; the cold wetted surface makes for quick setting and gives the finished dessert a glossy surface. Use pure olive oil to grease a metal mold.

5) To unmold, loosen the edges of the dessert with finger pressure. Invert the mold onto a plate or dish and jerk it to dislodge the contents. If the plate or dish is moistened with cold water, the desert can easily be moved to the right place.

Peach Condé

RICE AND OTHER WHOLE-GRAIN MOLDS

1 cup rice	Flavoring as
5 cups milk	below
⅜ cup sugar	1-2 tbs. unsalted
	butter (optional)

Rinse the rice and put it with the milk into a double saucepan or a thick pan, over a very low heat. Simmer very gently with the lid on the pan to prevent too much liquid evaporating. Stir occasionally to prevent the rice sticking to the bottom of the pan. Cook until it is tender and the milk has almost been absorbed. Sweeten, using sugar to suit your taste. Add flavoring, if you wish, and stir in the butter if you use it. Pour quickly into a cold wet bowl or mold. Turn out when set. Serve with stewed or canned fruit.

To flavor For chocolate flavor, add ½ cup cocoa to a spoonful of the warm milk. Mix to a creamy paste, then blend gradually with the rest of the milk; or add ⅜ cup coarsely grated chocolate to the hot milk before you turn the mixture into the mold. For coffee flavor, add coffee with the sugar, to suit your taste. For lemon or orange flavor, add finely-grated lemon or orange rind to the hot milk before molding the dessert, or soak thin strips of rind in it during the cooking; remove them before adding sugar and butter.

TO DECORATE

1) **Chocolate** Grate chocolate coarsely over the top.
2) **Coffee** Stir in coffee flavoring to taste.
3) **Orange** Stir in finely grated rind just before serving.
4) **Fruit** Fresh, canned, preserved, *or* stewed; e.g., peaches, pineapple, dessert apples, dates.
(*a*) Drain the fruit from the juice, chop or shred, and stir into the rice.
(*b*) Arrange fruit attractively on top of the rice, either in slices, quarters, halves or even a puree. The dish may be finished by piling a meringue on top and drying it to a golden brown in a cool oven (150 °C, 310 °F) or finished as for Peach Conde.

6 servings

CREAMED RICE

½ cup rice	1 tbs. sugar
2½ cups milk	2 tbs. sherry
1¼ cups heavy	(optional)
cream *or* ⅝ cup	
heavy cream and	
⅝ cup rich	
custard	

Cook the rice in the milk until tender. Drain in a colander set over a bowl until cold. Whip the cream until thick, and blend with the custard if used. Stir the rice, sugar, and the sherry, if you use it, into the cream mixture. Serve in individual stemmed glasses or dishes, and decorate with strips of glacé cherry or chopped preserved ginger.

6 servings

PEACH, APRICOT, OR PINEAPPLE CONDÉ

2½ cups cold rice	1 5-oz. can
mold	peaches, apricots,
¼ cup heavy	*or* pineapple
cream *or* cream	1 tsp. arrowroot
and custard	

Stir the cream into the cold rice mold to produce a soft, creamy consistency. Pour into serving dishes. Drain the fruit from the juice and arrange attractively on top of the rice. Make up the fruit juice to ⅝ cup with water. Blend the arrowroot with the fruit juice and boil until clear. Pour carefully over the fruit. Finish by decorating with whipped cream.

4 servings

SEMOLINA AND OTHER SMALL-GRAIN MOLDS

5 cups milk	Flavoring as
⅔ cup semolina	below
⅜ cup sugar	

Rinse a thick saucepan, put in the milk, and heat to boiling point. Sprinkle in the semolina, stirring as you do. Simmer, stirring all the time, until the grain is fully cooked and looks transparent when lifted on the back of a spoon (8-10 min.). Add the sugar and stir well. Pour quickly into a cold, wet mold.

TO FLAVOR

Chocolate Melt 3 oz. chocolate in the milk, or blend ³/₈ cup cocoa with some of the milk. Add rum, brandy, sherry, or vanilla extract.
Coffee Add 1 tbs. instant coffee with the sugar.
Lemon or Orange Infuse thin strips of rind with the milk while heating it. Remove before adding the grain.

6 servings   Cooking time – 10 min.
Setting time – 2 hr.

BANANA AND TAPIOCA SPONGE

6 bananas (not overripe)	2½ cups milk
¼ cup sugar	½ cup tapioca
⅝ cup water	Sugar to taste
Juice of ½ lemon	2-3 egg whites

Slice bananas and cook to a puree with the sugar and water (5-10 min.). Add strained lemon juice and beat to a smooth cream. Boil the milk, sprinkle in the tapioca, and cook gently for about 15 min., stirring constantly. Add banana puree; taste, and re-sweeten if necessary. Beat egg whites until stiff and fold lightly into the banana/tapioca mixture. Stir lightly until cool and serve piled up in a glass dish. Chill if liked.

6 servings   Cooking time – 35 min.

CARAMEL MOLD

1 lemon	½ cup ground rice
1 qt. milk	2 tbs. sugar

Caramel:

¼ cup sugar	1 tbs. cold water

Heat a charlotte or soufflé mold and have ready a thickly folded band of newspaper so that the hot pan may be encircled with it and held firmly in one hand. Melt sugar in the water in a thick, very small pan, and, when dissolved, boil quickly until it becomes dark golden brown. Do not stir. Pour at once into the hot tin mold, and rotate quickly to coat the sides and base of the mold. Finally, place mold on a firm flat board so that excess caramel may flow to the base and set level. Keep in a warm place, as drafts may cause the caramel coating to crack.

Cut thin strips of lemon rind and infuse slowly in the milk. Remove the rind when the milk boils; sprinkle in the rice, stirring all the time; cook until grain is soft and smooth, about 8-10 min. Sweeten to taste. Pour into the coated mold and leave in a cool place to set. Turn out and serve with cream.

6 servings

CRÈME DE RIZ

2½ cups milk	¼ cup sugar
⅓ cup ground rice	Flavoring
1½ tbs. powdered gelatin	⅝-1¼ cups heavy cream
2 tbs. cold water	

Heat the milk and, when boiling, sprinkle in the rice. Cook gently, stirring continuously until quite soft and smooth — 15-20 min. Avoid too much evaporation. Soak gelatin in the cold water, for 5-10 min., then warm until dissolved. Sweeten and flavor the rice, stir in the gelatin, and allow to cool, stirring lightly from time to time. When quite cool, but not set, fold in the whipped cream. Pour into a cold wet mold and allow to set.

This recipe can also be used for whole rice or semolina.

4 servings   Cooking time – ½ hr.
Setting time – 2 hr.

RIZ A L'IMPÉRATRICE

Make like Crème de Riz but set in an oiled border mold and decorate with fruit when turned out. Either: (*a*) fill the central hollow with fruit salad and piped whipped cream; *or* (*b*) place selected fruit, e.g., apricot halves, on the top of the border, glaze with apricot juice thickened with arrowroot (1 tsp. to 1¼ cups juice), and decorate with piped whipped cream and angelica.

TIMBALE OF SEMOLINA

1 qt. milk	2 tbs. powdered
⅔ cup finely	gelatin
ground	1¼ cups heavy
semolina	cream
4 tbs. water	

Filling:

2 dessert apples	5 tbs. apricot
2 ripe dessert	jam
pears	Lemon juice to
	taste

Heat the milk until boiling, then sprinkle on the semolina and stir in quickly. Heat at low heat, covered, for 10 min., stirring occasionally. Add the water to the powdered gelatin and dissolve over boiling water until it is liquid and clear. Add the gelatin to the semolina. Remove from the heat, and cool. Whip the cream until it holds its shape, and fold into the cooled semolina. Turn the mixture into a 5-cup ring mold, and allow to set in a cool place.

To make the filling, peel and core the apples and pears, and slice them thinly in wedge shapes. Heat gently in the apricot jam with lemon juice to taste until soft. Cool. When ready to serve, unmold the timbale carefully. Spoon the filling into the center of the ring. Serve with whipped cream if you wish.

6-7 servings

CORNSTARCH AND OTHER POWDERED-GRAIN MOLDS

¾ cup cornstarch	¼ cup sugar
5 cups milk	Flavoring

Blen cornstarch with a little cold milk to a thin cream. Boil remainder of milk and pour onto the blended cornstarch, stirring continuously. Return mixture to the pan and heat until boiling. Cook gently for 4 min., stirring all the time. Add sugar to taste, and flavoring, if used. Pour quickly into a wetted mold. Turn out when set.
Flavor with chocolate by blending ⅜ cup cocoa with the cornstarch and adding a few drops of vanilla or rum flavoring. Add extra sugar if needed. Flavor with coffee, lemon, or orange in the same way as

Semolina Mold.

6 servings *Cooking time – 15 min.*
Setting time – 2 hr.

AMROSIA MOLD

¾ cup cornstarch	½ cup sugar
5 cups milk	⅝ cup sherry
4 tbs. butter	

Blend cornstarch with a little of the milk to a thin cream. Boil rest of milk with the butter. Pour over blended cornstarch, return to pan, and cook thoroughly. Add sugar and sherry; pour into a moist mold. Turn out when cold; serve with wine sauce.

6 servings *Cooking time – 10 min.*
Setting time – 2 hr.

BUTTERSCOTCH MOLD

¼ cup cornstarch	2 tbs. butter
2½ cups milk	2 egg whites
⅝ cup brown	1 tsp. vanilla
sugar	extract

Blend cornstarch and make as for cornstarch mold. Melt the sugar in a heavy pan, stir in the butter, and pour into the cornstarch mixture. Beat well. Stiffly beat the egg whites and beat 2 tbs. into the cornstarch mixture to soften it a little. Fold in the remaining foam very lightly. Flavor with vanilla, and pile into a glass dish *or* mold, and chill.

6 servings *Cooking time – 20 min.*

FRUIT MOLD

2½ cups mixture as	1 cup stewed
for cornstarch	fruit
mold	

Put a thick layer of cornstarch mixture at the bottom of a mold. When set, place a tumbler in the center and fill the space between the 2 with cornstarch mixture. When the mixture is firm, remove the tumbler, fill the cavity with stewed fruit, and cover with a layer of cornstarch mixture. When set, turn out, and serve with custard or whipped cream.

5-6 servings *Time – about 2 hr.*

NEAPOLITAN MOLD

¾ cup cornstarch	Flavorings:
5 cups milk	almond,
1-2 tbs. butter	raspberry and
¼ cup sugar	coffee
Colorings:	
green, carmine	

Blend cornstarch and make like cornstarch mold. While cornstarch is cooking, warm 2 bowls. Sweeten cornstarch mixture to taste. Pour ⅓ quickly into a heated bowl, color pale pink, and flavor with raspberry flavoring. Stir quickly and pour into a moist mold. Pour ½ the remaining cornstarch mixture into a heated bowl, color pale green, and flavor with almond extract. Stir quickly and pour on the top of the set pink mixture. (This should be done lightly and slowly, pouring around the sides of the mold so that the second layer puts no great weight on the surface of the first.) Flavor the remaining ⅓ of the mixture with coffee flavoring and pour onto the set green mixture, again taking care not to pour too heavily. Let set, and turn out when cold.

6 servings   Cooking time – 20 min.
Setting time – 2 hr.

JUNKET

| 5 cups fresh milk | 2 tsp. rennet |
| 2 tsp. sugar | Flavoring |

Junkets are milk desserts set with rennet only, without either grain or gelatin. Warm the milk to lukewarm and stir in the sugar until dissolved. Add the rennet, stir, and pour at once into serving dishes. Put in a warm place to set. Serve with cream, if liked.

Chocolate Add 2-3 oz. plain chocolate, grated and dissolved in a little of the measured milk.

Coffee To milk add instant coffee powder to flavor, and decorate finished junket with chopped nuts.

Rum Add rum to taste.

Vanilla, Almond, Raspberry, etc. Add a few drops of extract.

Note: When using rennet in liquid or powder form, the manufacturer's instructions should always be followed carefully.
6 servings

Coffee Mousse and Junket

GELATIN DESSERTS, GENERAL HINTS

1) Make these desserts from fruit juices, fruit purees, flavored milk, or water and wine, with gelatin added. A gelatin dessert should only be set just enough to make it stand upright. If it is too stiff, it tastes rubbery. The gelatin sold in packets by manufacturers is carefully weighed to set to the right consistency in most weathers. In very hot weather you may need slightly more gelatin than stated on the packet.

To decorate a mold

Put 2 tbs. cold liquid jelly in mold and rotate to coat. Fix garnish in place with pins. Pour in a little more jelly to hold garnish. Fill mold when set. To unmold, invert and jerk to loosen.

2) You may also need more gelatin if the dessert:
(*a*) has pieces of fruit set in it
(*b*) is to be used for lining a mold
(*c*) is to be chopped for decoration
(*d*) is to be whipped and set as a "foam"

3) Use a metal mold if you can, as it gives a sharper outline to the gelatin when turned out. Tin-lined copper molds are expensive but give a perfect finish.

4) Make sure the mold is completely clean and free from grease if you want a sparkling gelatin dessert. A mold must be quite cold and should be rinsed with cold water just before you use it.

5) To unmold a gelatin, dip the mold quickly in very hot water up to its rim. Invert onto a cold, moist plate or dish, and jerk to dislodge the dessert.

To Clear Gelatin

To be sparklingly brilliant or to show off fruit and other decorations set in it, gelatin must be "cleared." Cleared gelatin is filtered through a foam of egg whites and crushed eggshells. The pan, beaters, and metal gelatin mold must first be scalded. The egg whites are lightly beaten until liquid, then added with the washed and crushed eggshells to the liquid gelatin dessert. The mixture is heated steadily and beaten constantly until a good head of foam is produced, and the contents of the pan are hot, but not quite boiling. As the hardened particles of egg white rise to the surface, they carry with them all the insoluble substances, forming a thick "crust" of foam. The correct temperature is reached

57

when the foam begins to set, so take care not to break it up, by beating too long a completely set foam. Remove the beaters, and heat to allow the foam crust to rise to the top of the pan. Then let the contents of the pan, covered with a lid, settle in a warm place for 5-10 min.

The gelatin is then poured through a scalded jelly cloth while the cloth is still hot, and into a scalded bowl below. The bowl of strained gelatin is replaced with another scalded bowl, and the gelatin is re-strained very carefully by pouring through the foam "crust" which covers the bottom of the cloth and acts as a filter.

Filtering is most easily carried out using a jelly bag and stand made for the purpose, but, if these are not available, the 4 corners of a clean cloth can be tied to the legs of an upturned stool and a bowl placed below the cloth.

For instructions on lining and garnishing a mold, see the captions to the pictures appearing on the previous page.

Whipped Gelatin Desserts

If gelatin is whipped or beaten just before setting, tiny bubbles of air are enclosed. These give a light texture, both stimulating and refreshing. The addition of egg white, slightly beaten and then whipped with the cold liquid gelatin increases the volume of the gelatin foam and also adds to its food value without unduly diluting the flavor, although a strongly flavored gelatin is needed if more than 1 egg white is used.

To Chop Gelatin

Use clear, sparkling gelatin, set very firm. Chop it with a wet knife on wet waxed paper. Chop coarsely; fine-chopped gelatin looks dulled.

AMBER GELATIN

1 pt. water	¾ cup sugar
½ cup sherry	3 tbs. gelatin
(optional)	3 egg yolks
⅝ cup lemon	Thin rind of
juice	1 lemon
(2 lemons)	

Put all ingredients into a pan and allow to soak 5 min. Beat over gentle heat until near boiling point. Do not boil, or the eggs will curdle. Strain through muslin and pour into a prepared mold.

4-6 servings   Cooking time – ½ hr.

BLACK CURRANT WHIP

⅝ cup black	1½ tbs. gelatin
currant puree	Sugar to taste
and 1¼ cups	
water *or* 2 cups	
black currant	
juice	

Heat the gelatin slowly in the juice *or* puree and water until dissolved. Add sugar if necessary. Cool, then beat briskly until a thick foam is produced. When the beater leaves a trail in the foam, pile quickly into a glass dish.

6 servings   Time – ½ hr.

BANANA CHARTREUSE

5 cups clear	1¼ cups heavy
lemon gelatin	cream
3 tbs. pistachio	Vanilla extract
nuts	Sugar to taste
4 bananas	

Line a 5-cup border mold with gelatin. Blanch, skin, chop, and dry the pistachio nuts, mix with 2 tbs. gelatin and run smoothly over the base of the mold. When set, cover with a ½-in. layer of clear gelatin. Slice a banana evenly, dip each slice in gelatin, and arrange them, slightly overlapping, in an even layer on the gelatin when set. Cover with another ½-in. layer of clear gelatin and allow to set. Repeat with fruit and gelatin until the mold is full, the last layer being gelatin. When set, turn out and pipe the whipped cream, sweetened, and flavored with vanilla, into the center. Surround with chopped gelatin.

6 servings
Setting time (without ice) – 2-3 hr.
(with ice) – ¾ hr.

CLARET GELATIN

4 lemons	Whites and shells
(⅝ cup juice)	of 2 eggs
3 cups water	¾ cup claret
¾ cup sugar	Carmine
4½ tbs. gelatin	

Use thinly cut rind of 2 lemons, and infuse with water, sugar, and gelatin. Add crushed shells and whites of eggs and lemon juice. Beat steadily until boiling point is almost reached. Remove beaters and boil to the top of the pan. Pour in the claret without disturbing the foam "crust." Boil again to the top of the pan. Remove from the heat, cover, and let settle for 1 min. Filter, then add the color, drop by drop; cool; remove froth; mold in scalded individual molds.

4-6 servings   Time – 45 min.

COFFEE WHIP

2½ cups milk	2¼ tbs. gelatin
1 tbs. instant	soaked and
coffee powder	dissolved in 4
Sugar to taste	tbs. water
	1-2 egg whites
	(optional)

Decoration:

Chopped nuts

Heat together the milk, coffee, and sugar. Heat the gelatin in the water until dissolved, then cool slightly. Add to the cooled coffee-flavored milk and beat. If egg whites are used, beat them until liquid and slightly frothy, and stir into the cool gelatin just before beating. When thick, pile into a dish and scatter chopped nuts over the top.

6 servings   Cooking time – 10 min.
Setting time – ½ hr.

DUTCH FLUMMERY

1 lemon	½ cup sherry *or*
2½ cups water	Madeira
3 tbs. gelatin	Sugar to taste
2 eggs	

Wash lemon and cut thin strips of rind; infuse the rind in water. Add gelatin and simmer gently until dissolved. Beat the eggs, add wine, juice of the lemon, and water with the gelatin. Strain all into a pan and stir over gentle heat until thick. Sweeten to taste and pour into a 5 cup moist mold. Turn out when set.

6 servings   Cooking time – about 40 min.
Setting time – 2-3 hr.

HONEYCOMB MOLD

5 cups milk	2 large eggs
Flavoring:	2 tbs. sugar
vanilla extract *or*	1½ tbs. gelatin
lemon *or* orange	4 tbs. water
rind	

If orange or lemon rind is being used for flavoring, slowly infuse thinly cut strips of rind in the milk. Remove the rind and make a custard with the egg yolks, sugar and flavored milk. If using vanilla extract, add to the custard after the sugar. Dissolve gelatin in measured water and, while still warm, stir into the custard. Allow to cool. When just beginning to set, fold in the stiffly beaten egg whites. Pour into a quart border mold and allow to set. Turn out and serve with fruit salad piled up in the hollow. Decorate with whipped cream.

4-6 servings

FRUIT IN GELATIN

3¾ cup very clear	Selected pieces of
lemon *or*	fruit, e.g. bananas,
wine gelatin,	black and
using white	green grapes,
wine instead of	tangerines,
sherry and	cherries, apricot,
brandy	pineapple, etc.

Scald a metal mold, then rinse it with cold water. Cover the bottom with a thin layer of cool gelatin (about ⅛ in. thick). Avoid the formation of bubbles in the gelatin by tilting the mold and placing the gelatin in spoonfuls in the bottom. Bubbles will spoil the clear transparency of the gelatin when turned out. If they do form, remove with a teaspoon. Allow to set. Cut pieces of fruit to suit the hollows and spaces of the mold, dip each piece into cold liquid gelatin, and set in place around and on the gelatin layer. Let set and cover carefully with a layer of clear gelatin. Allow to set. Repeat, taking care that each layer of fruit is quite firm before adding a layer of gelatin — otherwise the fruit may be "floated" from its position. Fill the mold to the top. When set, turn out and decorate with piped cream *or* chopped clear gelatin.

6 servings   Time (without ice) – 3-4 hr.
(with ice packed around the mold) – 1 hr.

LEMON CURD GELATIN

3 large lemons	3 tbs. gelatin
3¾ cups milk	(lightweight)
1 cup sugar	4 tbs. water

Wash lemons and remove rind in thin strips from 2 of them. Infuse rind in the milk with the sugar until the latter is dissolved. Soak the gelatin in the water and, when soft, stir into the warm milk. Do not allow the milk with gelatin, to boil or curdling may occur. Strain into a bowl, and allow to cool to lukewarm. Stir in the strained juice of 3 lemons, and mold. Turn out when set.

Note: If curdling should occur, beat vigorously before molding and a fine, spongy texture will be formed.

6 servings   Cooking time – ½ hr.
Setting time – 2 hr.

LEMON GELATIN

4 lemons	1-in. cinnamon
Sherry (optional)	stick
3¾ cups water	5-6 tbs. gelatin
¾ cup sugar	Shells and whites
4 cloves	of 2 eggs

Scald a large pan, beaters, and metal gelatin mold. Wash lemons and cut thin strips of rind, avoiding white pith. Extract juice, and measure. Make up to 1¼ cups with water *or* sherry, but if the latter is used, do not add until just before clearing the gelatin. Put the 3¾ cups water, 1¼ cups juice, rinds, sugar, flavorings, and gelatin into the scalded pan and infuse, with a lid on, over gentle heat until sugar and gelatin are dissolved. Do not let the infusion become hot. Wash egg shells, and crush. Lightly beat the whites until liquid and add, with shells, to the infusion. Heat steadily, beating constantly, until a good head of foam is produced and the contents of the pan become hot, but not quite boiling. Strain through the crust (*see* p. 58), and add sherry, if used, to the gelatin as it goes through the filter.

6 servings   Time – 1-1½ hr.

ORANGE GELATIN

2½ cups water	2 lemons
⅜-½ cup sugar	Angelica
4½ tbs. gelatin	(optional)
6 oranges (2½ cups juice)	

Put water, sugar, and gelatin into a pan. Wash fruit and cut thin strips of outer rind from 3 oranges, avoiding white pith. Add strips to the pan and bring slowly to a boil. Leave to infuse, with the lid on, for 10 min. Squeeze juice from oranges and lemons and strain onto juice. Then, *(a)* pour into a wet metal mold; *or (b)* prepare orange-skin "cups" made from half-sections of peel freed from pulp. Fill with liquid gelatin, stand in patty shell or muffin pans to hold upright until set, and decorate with piped cream and angelica-strip "handles" to form baskets; *or (c)* allow to set in orange-skin cups, then cut the halves into quarters and arrange as boats.

6 servings   Cooking time – 10 min.
Setting time – 2 hr.

PINEAPPLE WHIP

1 pt. pineapple juice	1½ tbs. gelatin

Proceed as for Black Currant Whip.

PORT WINE GELATIN

2½ cups water	3 tbs. gelatin
¼ cup sugar	1¼ cups port
2 tbs. red currant jelly	wine
	Red food coloring

Put water, sugar, red currant jelly, and gelatin into a pan and let soak for 5 min. Heat slowly until dissolved. Add ½ the port wine and color dark red with a few drops of red food coloring. Strain through double muslin; add the rest of the wine. Pour into a wet mold.

6 servings   Cooking time – 10 min.
Setting time – 2 hr.

ORANGE CUSTARD GELATIN

5 oranges	2⅓ tbs. gelatin
½ cup sugar	2 eggs

Wash oranges and cut rind from 2-in. thin strips. Strain orange juice and make up to 3¾ cups with water. Add rind, sugar, and gelatin and heat gently until dissolved. Allow to cool, and add well-beaten eggs. Cook again to thicken, but do not boil. Strain into a wet 5-cup mold. Turn out when set.

6 servings   Cooking time – about 45 min.
Setting time – 2 hr.

Cold Soufflés, Creams, and Trifles

Cold soufflés and mousses are very like whipped gelatins, being beaten, and usually set with gelatin. But they have a custard base to hold the flavoring and as a rule contain whipped cream. They can be rich as well as light, a party dessert that any hostess can offer with pleasure. Creams and bavarois (Bavarian creams or half-creams) are like soufflés without the quantity of egg whites. Full creams consist simply of cream and flavorings set with gelatin, and are very rich. However, many people prefer the more subtle flavors of bavarois in which a rich custard is combined with the cream. A bavarois is the basis of many familiar party desserts, such as Charlotte Russe.

Trifles are a typical English dessert. They consist mainly of sponge cake and fruit or liqueur flavoring, soaked with custard, and topped with cream. There are many different trifles, and some of them have a long history under other names.

COLD SOUFFLÉS AND MOUSSES, GENERAL HINTS

1) Prepare a soufflé dish before you begin making a soufflé. Tie a double band of waxed paper around a straight-sided dish or a charlotte mold so that 2½-3 in. paper rises above the rim. The soufflé mixture should come at least 1 in. above the rim, so that

when the paper is taken off, the soufflé appears to have risen above the top of the dish.

2) While making the soufflé, keep the mixture warm but never let it get really hot. It would cook the egg and prevent it entrapping air.

3) Half-whip the cream to the same consistency as the custard, and beat the egg whites to match them. It makes blending the mixtures much easier.

MILANAISE SOUFFLÉ
(Basic Cold Soufflé Recipe)

2 lemons	1½ tbs. gelatin
4 eggs	⅝ cup water
⅝ cup sugar	

For Decoration:

Chopped nuts, preferably pistachio	Whipped cream or apple slices (optional)

Grate the rind of the lemons. Squeeze the juice. Half-whip the cream and whip the egg whites. Beat the egg yolks, rind, and sugar over hot water until beginning to get thick. Trickle in the lemon juice and continue beating until the mixture is thick. Remove from the heat. Soften the gelatin in the water, then warm it to dissolve it. Pour the gelatin into the custard slowly, and stir it in lightly. Fold in the cream, then the egg whites as lightly as possible. Keep the bowl on ice as you do so if the mixture seems at all likely to separate. Pour the mixture into the prepared soufflé dish, and allow to set. When set and ready to be used, dip a knife in hot water and slide it between the soufflé and the paper rim. Ease the soufflé away from the paper. Remove the paper. Decorate the sides of the soufflé with chopped nuts, then top with cream and fruit if you wish.

VARIATIONS

Apricot Soufflé Use 1¼ cups apricot puree and a few drops of red food coloring in place of lemon rind and juice. Use only 4 tbs. water.

Orange Soufflé Use the rind and juice of 3 oranges and the rind of ½ lemon instead of the rind and juice of 2 lemons.

Raspberry or Strawberry Soufflé Use 1¼ cups fruit puree and a few drops of food coloring in place of the lemon rind and juice.

6 servings   Setting time – 2 hr.

MILK CHOCOLATE SOUFFLÉ

2 eggs	2 oz. milk chocolate
¼ cup sugar	
12 tbs. evaporated milk	1½ tbs. gelatin
	4 tbs. warm water

For Decoration:

Whipped cream

Put egg yolks and sugar in a double saucepan and beat until thick and creamy. Whip the evaporated milk until thick, and add to the eggs and sugar. Melt the chocolate over very low heat; add to the egg and sugar mixture. Put the gelatin in the warm water and heat to dissolve, then stir it into the chocolate mixture. Whip up the egg whites until stiff, and stir into the chocolate mixture. Put into the prepared soufflé case. When set, remove the paper carefully, and decorate the top with cream.

6 servings   Setting time – 2 hr.

CHOCOLATE MOUSSE

4 eggs	3 tbs. strong black coffee
½ cup sugar	
¼ cup frozen concentrated orange juice	¾ cup soft unsalted butter
	Pinch of salt
6 oz. plain dark chocolate	1 tbs. sugar

Separate the eggs. Beat the yolks and

sugar together until thick and pale. Beat in the orange juice. Place the bowl over very hot but not boiling water and stir or beat, clearing the sides of the bowl, until the mixture thickens evenly and is too hot to touch. Remove from the heat, place on ice or over cold water, and beat until cooled and like thick mayonnaise. Melt the chocolate over hot water. Remove from heat, and beat in the butter gradually, making a smooth cream. Stir the chocolate lightly into the egg and sugar. Beat the egg whites until firm. Sprinkle on the salt and a tbs. sugar; beat again until stiff. Stir 1 tbs. into the chocolate mixture. Then fold in the remainder. Turn into a prepared soufflé dish and allow to set. Prepare for serving like a Milanaise Soufflé, but decorate with whipped cream only.

8 servings

VELVET CREAM (Basic Full Cream)

¾ tbs. gelatin	Sherry *or* vanilla
4 tbs. water	extract
3-4 tbs. sugar	2½ cups heavy
	cream

Soak the gelatin in the cold water for 5 min. Heat gently until dissolved and clear. Stir in the sugar until dissolved. Add the sherry or vanilla. Whip the cream until thick, and fold into it the flavored liquid gelatin. Pour into a prepared mold to set.
6 servings   Setting time – 1 hr.

VARIATION

Pistachio Cream Instead of sherry or vanilla extract use ¾ cup chopped pistachio nuts and a little green coloring.

CHOCOLATE BAVAROIS OR BAVARIAN CREAM (Half-Cream)

4 oz. plain	¼-⅜ cup sugar
chocolate	1½ tbs. gelatin
1¼ cups milk	4 tbs. water
3 egg yolks *or* 1	1 tsp. vanilla *or*
whole egg and 1	coffee flavoring
yolk	1¼ cups heavy
	cream

Grate the chocolate and dissolve it in the milk. Beat eggs and sugar until liquid, and make a thick pouring custard with the fla-

vored milk, straining back into the pan to cook and thicken. Do not allow to boil, or the eggs may curdle. Allow to cool. Soak gelatin in the water for 5 min., then heat to dissolve. Stir the vanilla or coffee flavoring gently into the cooled custard, and add the dissolved gelatin, stirring again as it cools. Whip the cream and fold lightly into the custard mixture just before setting. Pour into a prepared mold or into glass dishes.
6 servings   Setting time – 1-2 hr.

COFFEE BAVARIAN CREAM

3 egg yolks *or*	1½ tbs. gelatin
1 whole egg	4 tbs. water
and 1 yolk	½ cup strong
¼-½ cup sugar	coffee
1¼ cups milk	1¼ cups heavy
	cream

Beat the eggs and sugar until liquid. Heat the milk almost to boiling point and pour over the egg mixture. Strain the egg and milk back into the pan and cook gently until thick, stirring all the time. Allow to cool. Soak the gelatin in the water for 5 min., then heat to dissolve. Stir the coffee into the cooled custard, and add the dissolved gelatin, stirring again as it cools. Whip the cream and fold lightly into the custard mixture just before setting. Pour into a prepared mold or into glass dishes.
6 servings   Setting time – 1-2 hr.

FRUIT BAVARIAN CREAM (Basic Recipe for All Fruit Half-Creams)

1¼ cups fruit	1½ tbs. gelatin
puree	4 tbs. water *or*
1¼ cups thick,	thin fruit juice
rich custard	Coloring
Sugar to sweeten	(optional)
Lemon juice	1¼ cups heavy
(optional)	cream

Puree the fruit through a very fine sieve — nylon mesh if possible. Blend with the cool custard, sweeten, and flavor with lemon juice if desired. Soak the gelatin in the water or juice for a few min., and heat to dissolve. Pour, while steaming hot, into the custard and fruit mixture, and stir to keep well-blended until the mixture begins to feel heavy and drags on

Milanaise Soufflé

Fruit Bavarian Cream
in a Crumb Crust

the spoon. Color if necessary. Lightly stir in the whipped cream and pour into a prepared mold.

Note: apricots, black currants, damsons, gooseberries, greengages, peaches, raspberries, *or* strawberries can be used for the puree.

6 servings   Setting time – 1-2 hr.

GARIBALDI CREAM

1¼ cups strawberry cream	1¼ cups pistachio cream
1¼ cups vanilla cream	(*see* **Velvet Cream**)

Place the strawberry cream at the bottom of a prepared mold. Allow to set. Add the vanilla cream and set. Put the pistachio cream on top. Turn out and surround with chopped gelatin.

6 servings   Setting time (with ice) – 45 min.
(without ice) – 3-2 hr.

GINGER CREAM

¼-½ cups chopped preserved ginger	1½ tbs. gelatin
1¼ cups milk	4 tbs. water
3 egg yolks	2-3 tbs. ginger syrup
Sugar to taste	1¼ cups heavy cream

Infuse the preserved ginger in the milk. Beat the eggs and sugar until liquid, and make a thick pouring custard with the flavored milk, straining back into the pan to cook and thicken. Allow to cool. Soak gelatin in the water for 5 min., then heat to dissolve. Stir the ginger syrup gently into the cooled custard, and add the dissolved gelatin, stirring again as it cools. Whip the cream and fold lightly into a prepared mold or into glass dishes.

6 servings   Setting time (with ice) – 45 min.
(without ice) – 1-2 hr.

ITALIAN BAVAROIS OR CREAM

1 lemon	¼-½ cup sugar
1¼ cups milk	1½ tbs. gelatin
3 egg yolks *or*	¼ cup water
1 whole egg and 1 yolk	1¼ cups heavy cream

Infuse thin strips of lemon rind in the milk. Beat eggs and sugar until liquid, and make a thick pouring custard with the flavored milk, straining back into the pan to cook and thicken. Allow to cool. Soak gelatin in the water for 5 min., then heat to dissolve. Stir juice of lemon into the cooled custard, and add the dissolved gelatin stirring again as it cools. Whip the cream and fold lightly into the custard mixture just before setting. Pour into a prepared mold and let set. If you like, the cream can be poured into individual glass dishes and decorated according to taste.

6 servings   Setting time – 1-2 hr.

ORANGE CREAM

3 large oranges	¼ cup sugar
1¼ cups milk	2⅓ tbs. gelatin
3 egg yolks	⅝ cup heavy cream

Infuse thin strips of rind from 2 oranges in the milk. Remove the rind and make into a thick pouring custard with the egg yolks and sugar. Soak the gelatin in the orange juice and add sufficient water to make 1¼ cups. Heat to dissolve, and strain into the orange-flavored custard. Whip the cream and fold in when the gelatin-custard mixture is thick but not set. Pour into a prepared mold and turn out when quite cold.

6 servings   Setting time – 1-2 hr.

QUEEN MAB'S PUDDING

2½ cups milk	4 tbs. water
3 eggs	⅜ cup glacé cherries
⅜ cup sugar	
Vanilla extract	3 tbs. citron peel
1½ tbs. gelatin	⅝ cup heavy cream

Make a custard with the milk, eggs, and sugar; flavor with vanilla. Soak gelatin in the water for 5 min., then heat until dissolved. Stir into the custard. Cut cherries in halves and shred the peel. Stir into the custard and, lastly, fold in the cream, whipped to a consistency similar to that of the cool custard. Just before setting, pour into a prepared mold. Turn out when set.

6 servings   Setting time – 1-2 hr.

PINEAPPLE BAVARIAN

1 tbs. plain gelatin	1 cup whipping cream
1/4 cup cold water	juice of 1 lemon (3 tbs.)
1 flat can crushed pineapple (1 1/3 cups)	1/4 cup sugar

Soften the gelatin in the cold water for 5 min. Drain the juice from the pineapple and heat to boiling; stir in the gelatin until dissolved and let cool. Beat cream in chilled bowl until fluffy, add lemon juice and sugar and beat until stiff. Fold in gelatin mixture and crushed pineapple. Cover and chill until firm.

3 servings   Setting time – 1-2 hr.

RUM BAVARIAN CREAM

1 bay leaf	1 1/2 tbs. gelatin
1 1/4 cups milk	4 tbs. water
3 egg yolks *or* 1 whole egg and 1 yolk	1/2 cup rum 1 1/4 cups heavy cream
1/4-1/2 cup sugar	

Infuse the bay leaf in the milk for 20 min. Beat eggs and sugar until liquid and make a thick pouring custard with the flavored milk, straining back into the pan to cook and thicken. Allow to cool. Soak gelatin in the water for 5 min., then heat to dissolve. Stir the dissolved gelatin into the cooled custard. Stir in the rum. Whip the cream and fold lightly into the custard mixture just before setting. Pour into a prepared mold or into glass dishes.

6 servings   Setting time – 1-2 hr.

VANILLA BAVAROIS OR CREAM

3 egg yolks *or* 1 whole egg and 1 yolk	1 1/2 tbs. gelatin 4 tbs. water 2 tsp. vanilla extract
1/4-1/2 cup sugar	
1 1/4 cups milk	1 1/4 cups heavy cream

Beat the eggs and sugar until liquid. Heat the milk to almost boiling and pour over the egg mixture. Strain the egg and milk back into the saucepan and cook very gently until thick, stirring all the time. Allow to cool. Soak the gelatin in the water for 5 min., then heat to dissolve. Stir the vanilla extract into the cooled custard, and add the dissolved gelatin, stirring again as it cools. Whip the cream and fold lightly into the custard mixture just before setting. Pour into a prepared mold or into glass dishes.

6 servings   Setting time – 1-2 hr.

COLD CHARLOTTES, GENERAL HINTS

Most cold charlottes are half-creams surrounded by lady or sponge or similar cakes. You can line the charlotte mold with these before pouring in the cream mixture. For a perfect, unsmeared "fit," it is usually easier to stick them on the outside of the cream after unmolding it. The great Carême invented these cold desserts.

CHARLOTTE A LA ST. JOSÉ

20 ladyfingers	3 3/4 cups pineapple Bavarian *or* custard

Decoration:	
Preserved pineapple	1/2 pkg. lemon gelatin

Prepare lemon gelatin according to pkg. directions. Line the bottom of a mold with the gelatin, and, when set, decorate with fancily cut pieces of preserved pineapple dipped in gelatin. Allow to set, then cover with another thin layer of cold liquid gelatin. When the gelatin has set, line the sides of the mold with ladyfingers, with the ends trimmed so that they fit closely onto the gelatin. Remove any crumbs from the surface of the gelatin with the tip of a dry pastry brush. Pour the pineapple custard into the lined mold and let set. Trim the fingers level with the rim. Turn out, and decorate with piped cream.

CHARLOTTE RUSSE

20 ladyfingers	1 qt. Italian cream

Coat the bottom of a mold with gelatin.

When the gelatin has set, line the sides of the mold with ladyfingers, with the ends trimmed so that they fit closely onto the gelatin. Remove any crumbs from the surface of the gelatin with the tip of a dry pastry brush. Pour the cream mixture into the lined mold and let set. Trim the fingers level with the rim. Turn out, and decorate with piped cream.

If you prefer, line the base of the mold with sponge cake.

6 servings

APRICOT TRIFLE

5-6 slices Swiss	2½ cups custard
Jam Roll	½ pt. cream
1-2 Macaroons	1 tsp. gelatin
2-3 tbs. sherry	2 tsp. boiling
1 8-oz. can	water
apricots	

Cut the Jam Roll into small cubes and place with broken macaroons in the bottom of a shallow glass dish; pour the sherry and a little apricot juice over. Cut up some of the apricots and add to the dish; pour over the custard. Allow to set. Whip the cream, adding the gelatin melted in the water. Pile the cream so that it is fairly high in the center. Decorate with apricots.

SWISS CREAM OR TRIFLE

¼ lb. Ratafia	¼ cup sugar
Biscuits *or* sponge	¾-1¼ cups heavy
cake	cream
3-4 tbs. sherry	2 tsp. chopped *or*
5 tbs. cornstarch	grated nuts *or*
2½ cups milk	glacé
1 lemon	fruits

Put the Ratafia Biscuits or cake in the bottom of a glass dish, or individual dishes, and soak with sherry. Blend the cornstarch with sufficient milk to make a smooth cream. Heat the rest of the milk at low heat with thin strips of lemon rind. Strain onto the blended cornstarch, return to the pan, and cook thoroughly but gently for 3-4 min. Stir in the sugar. Allow to cool. Whip the cream slightly and add it and the juice of the lemon and gradually to the cool cornstarch cream. Re-sweeten if

necessary. Pour over the soaked biscuits or cake and chill. Decorate with chopped nuts, or glacé cherries and thinly cut strips of angelica.

4-6 servings   Cooking time – 25 min.

ST. HONORÉ TRIFLE

1 round sponge	¼ lb. Macaroons
cake (1 in. thick	*or* Ratafia Biscuits
by 6 in. across)	⅝ cup sherry
2-3 egg whites	1¼ cups heavy
½ cup sugar	cream

For Decoration:

Glacé cherries	Angelica

Place sponge cake on a baking sheet. Make meringue with egg whites and sugar. Pipe a border of meringue around the top edge of the sponge cake, and dry in a very cool oven (135 °C, 265 °F). Do not allow meringue to color. Place a thick layer of macaroons *or* ratafias on top of the cake and soak well with the sherry for at least 1 hr. Avoid touching the meringue with sherry — it may crumble. Pile whipped cream on top, and decorate with cherries and angelica.

6 servings

TRADITIONAL TRIFLE or DEAN'S CREAM

4 individual	3 tbs. almonds
sponge cakes	(blanched and
Raspberry or	shredded)
strawberry jam	1¼ cups custard
Marmalade	using 1¼ cups
6 Macaroons	milk, 1 egg,
12 Ratafia Biscuits	and 1 egg yolk
⅝ cup sherry	¾ cup heavy
Grated rind of	cream
½ lemon	1 egg white
	2-4 tbs. sugar.

For Decoration:

Glacé cherries	Angelica

Cut the sponge cakes in half horizontally and spread the cut sides alternately with jam and marmalade. Arrange in a glass dish with the jam and marmalade showing through. Fill the center of the dish with

Garibaldi Cream

Charlotte Russe

Macaroons and Ratafias. Soak them with sherry, and sprinkle with lemon rind and almonds. Cover with the custard and allow to cool. Beat the cream, egg white, and sugar together until stiff. Pile on top of the triffle. Decorate with the cherries and angelica.

6 servings

TIPSY CAKE

1 sponge cake
  or 8 individual
  cakes
Raspberry jam
	⅜ cup Madeira
	  or sherry

For Decoration:

Almonds	Glacé cherries

Split the cake or cakes and spread ½ thickly with jam. Sandwich together again and place in a dish. Pour over the wine and allow to soak for 1 hr. Pour over the custard, stick the blanched almonds in like a porcupine, and decorate with cherries and angelica.

6-7 servings

Meringue Nests

Meringue and Fruit Desserts

MERINGUE SHELLS

4 eggs	1 cup sugar

Make sure the egg whites are fresh and contain no trace of yolk or grease. Break down with a beater or wire whisk to an even-textured liquid by tapping lightly for a few moments. Then beat evenly and continuously until a firm, stiff, close-textured foam is obtained. Beat in 1 tbs. sugar. Add the rest of the sugar, a little at a time, by folding it in lightly with a metal spoon.

For a single large meringue shell or case make a circle in pencil on waxed paper. Cover the pencil line with a layer of meringue. Pipe a "wall" of meringue around the edge with a pastry bag. For small meringue shells force through a ⅜-in. pipe into small rounds; *or* form into egg shapes with two spoons dipped in cold water, and place on strips of oiled kitchen paper on baking sheets. In either case, dredge well with sugar and dry in a cool oven (140 °C, 290 °F), placed low to avoid discoloring, and reduce to 130 °C, 265 °F, after 1 hr. If a pure white meringue is required, *very* slow drying is essential, by leaving the meringue in a barely warm oven overnight.

VARIATION

Meringue Nests Make in the same way as the large meringue shell, but in a much smaller size for individual helpings.

Note: Meringue for topping fruit dishes may be required less sweet. If so, beat only ½ the sugar into the stiff foam. Then pile the mixture on the dessert, dust lightly with sugar, and bake in a cool oven at 140 °C, 290 °F, for 30-40 min.

MERINGUE GÂTEAU OR VACHERIN WITH STRAWBERRIES

6 egg whites	Sugar
1½ cups sugar	¾-1¼ cups heavy
1½ lb. strawberries	cream
Juice of 1 lemon	

Make the meringue as above. Put into a plain forcing pipe (½ in.) and pipe a round base, working from the center outward, 6 in. in diameter. Build up the sides to 1½ in. high. Pipe the remaining meringue into small shell shapes. Bake in a very cool oven (130 °C, 250 °F), then cool.

Prepare strawberries, sprinkle with lemon juice and sugar, and allow to stand until meringue shell is ready. Reserve choice fruits for decoration; place the rest in the

Meringue desserts

Fruit Salad in a
pineapple shell

Pear and
Raspberry Pavlova

meringue shell. Cover with the whipped cream. Decorate with meringue shells and strawberries.

PEAR AND RASPBERRY PAVLOVA

3 egg whites	1 pear, peeled,
3/4 cups sugar	cored, and sliced
1 tsp. cornstarch	Juice of 1/2 lemon
sifted	Frozen *or* fresh
1 1/4 cups heavy	raspberries
cream	

Beat the egg whites until they form peaks. Then beat in 1/2 the sugar until stiff. Fold in the remaining sugar and the cornstarch. Pile meringue mixture into a shallow baking dish, hollowing out the center to form a flan shell. Bake in a slow oven, 130 °C, 250 °F, for 1 1/2 hr. Allow to cool. Marinate pear slices in lemon juice. Whip cream, and fill center of pavlova. Arrange pears and raspberries on top.

FRUIT PUREES (for all desserts)

Fruit purees for all sweet dishes, including creams, ice creams, and sauces, are made by rubbing fresh, frozen, or canned fruit through a fine sieve, or by using an electric blender. Fruit containing seeds or stones must be sieved before blending. A nylon sieve should always be used.

FRUIT SALAD

3/8 cup granulated	1 cup green
sugar	grapes
1 1/4 cups water	1 small can
3 oranges	pineapple
Rind and juice	segments
of 1 lemon	3 red-skinned
3 ripe dessert	dessert apples
pears	

Bring the sugar and water to a boil together with strips of rind taken from 1 orange and the lemon. Cool. Sieve to remove the rind. Cut up the oranges, removing the skin and white pith, and section out the flesh, removing the seeds. Halve the grapes, removing the seeds. Place these in the cooled sugar and water. Empty the pineapple pieces and juice into the fruit salad. Refrigerate if possible.

Just before serving, quarter, core and slice the apples thinly and toss in the lemon juice. Dice the pears and also toss in lemon juice. Add these to the fruit salad. Arrange attractively in a suitable serving dish. Chill and serve.

Fresh pineapple and canned mandarin segments are attractively colored fruit to use. Try piling the salad in a shell or half-shell of pineapple.

STEWED FRUIT OR FRUIT FOOL

Fresh or dried	Flavoring of
fruit as below	lemon *or* orange
Sugar, as below	rind, claret,
	sherry, *or* 1 *or* 2
	cloves

The amount of sugar needed will depend on the sweetness of the fruit. Dried fruit usually needs only 2-4 tbs. per lb.; tart gooseberries may need 1/4-1/2 cup. The amount of water varies likewise. Forced rhubarb needs little or none, but apples and pears should be covered to keep them white. Leave small, fresh apples and pears whole; cut large ones into quarters. Place immediately in syrup (see below) to prevent them becoming brown. Cloves flavor apples well.

Gooseberries, plums, and any tart stone fruit should be de-stalked; take out the stones or not as you wish. Cook very slowly until the skins crack.

To stew any fruit, make a syrup by dissolving the sugar in water. Add the flavoring and fruit. Cook either on top of the stove, just below boiling, or in a warm oven. When the fruit is cooked, drain it and pile it in a serving dish. Boil the syrup to make it thick, cool it, and pour it over the fruit.

To make a classic fruit fool, sieve the drained fruit or process it in an electric blender after removing the stones, if necessary. Make 2 1/2 cups thick pouring custard per 1 1/2 lb. fruit *or* use 2 1/2 cups whipped heavy cream (or 1 1/4 cups cream and 1 1/4 cups custard). Make the fruit puree the same consistency as the cream, by adding a little fruit syrup if necessary. Blend the 2 mixtures.

Pastries, Large and Small

Many pies, flans, and tarts are made to be eaten cold. Some have fillings set with gelatin or with cream or custard; all are popular desserts.

We also bake a great many small tartlets and pastries of widely varied kinds. Some of these are traditional to our old folk festivals, others have been created for aristocrats and stage stars. We eat them on hundreds of different occasions, from children's parties to wedding buffets.

APPLE MERINGUE FLAN

Pâte sucrée, using 1 cup flour, etc.	¼ cup margarine
4-5 medium cooking apples	⅜ cup brown sugar
2 tbs. water	2 eggs
Rind of ½ lemon	¼-½ cup sugar for meringue

Peel, core, and slice the apples; put them in a saucepan and stew with the water and the finely grated lemon rind. When soft, pass through a nylon sieve. Return the apple pulp to the pan and reheat slightly, add the butter, brown sugar, and egg yolks. Meanwhile, line a 7-in. flan ring with the pastry. Put the apple mixture into the uncooked lined flan ring and bake in a moderate oven (180 °C, 350 °F) for about 30 min., until the apple mixture is set. Stiffly beat the egg whites and fold in ¼-½ cup sugar. Pile on top of the apple mixture, dredge lightly with sugar, and decorate, if liked, with pieces of angelica and glacé cherry. Bake in a very cool oven (145 °C, 290 °F) until the meringue is golden brown, about 30-40 min.

Note: A good pinch of ground cinnamon and ground cloves can be added to the apples before the butter, sugar, and egg yolks, if liked.

6-7 servings

75

BEATRICE TARTLETS

Pâte sucrée,	3 tbs. chopped
using 1½ cups	walnuts
flour, etc.	5/8 cup heavy
3 bananas	cream
Juice of 1 lemon	1 oz. finely
1½ tbs. sugar	grated chocolate

Line 12 patty shells with Pâte Sucrée , and bake them "blind" in a moderate oven (180°C, 350 °F). Allow to cool. Chop the bananas with the lemon juice and add sugar and walnuts. Pile the mixture into the tartlet shells. Pipe a large rosette of sweetened whipped cream on top, and dredge with chocolate.

12 tartlets   Cooking time – 15 min.

CREAM BUNS

Choux Pastry,	Confectioners' sugar
using ½ cup	
flour, etc.	

Filling:

1¼ cups sweetened heavy cream flavored with vanilla extract *or* **confectioner's custard,** *or* **mock cream may be used**

1) Put the pastry into a forcing bag and pipe balls onto a greased baking sheet, using a 1-in. vegetable pipe, or shape the mixture with a spoon into piles and bake in a fairly hot oven (220 °C, 425 °F) for 30 min. (do not open the door), then move to

Apple Meringue Flan

a cooler part of the oven for about 10 min., until dried inside. Split the buns and remove any damp mixture. When cold, fill with whipped cream and dust with confectioners' sugar.

12 buns   Cooking time – 40 min.

CUSTARD PIE

Shortcrust	1 egg yolk
pastry, using	1½ tbs. sugar
1 cup flour,	1¼ cups milk
etc.	Grated nutmeg
1 egg	

Line a 7-in. flan ring with shortcrust pastry. Bake "blind." Beat the eggs and add to them the sugar and warmed milk. Strain into the flan shell, sprinkle with grated nutmeg, and bake in a warm oven until set (140 °C, 335 °F).

5-6 servings   Cooking time – 30-40 min.

DAMSON TART

Shortcrust	3¾ cups damsons
pastry, using	½ cup brown
1½ cups flour,	sugar
etc.	

Half-fill an 8-in. pie dish with damsons; sprinkle on the sugar; pile the remaining damsons on top, piling them high in the center. Line the edges of the dish with pastry and cover it with pastry, brush lightly over with cold water, dredge with sugar, and bake in a fairly hot oven (200 °C, 400 °F).

5-6 servings   Cooking time – about 1 hr.

ÉCLAIRS

Choux Pastry	Sugar to sweeten
1¼ cups heavy	Vanilla extract
cream *or*	Chocolate *or*
confectioner's	Coffee Glacé
custard *or* mock	Icing
cream	

Grease a baking sheet. Place the pastry in a pastry bag with a large plain pipe (¾ in. to 1 in.) and pipe mixture onto the greased

Cream Buns

sheet in 4-in. lengths, cutting off each length with a knife dipped in hot water. Bake in a hot oven (220 °C, 400°-425°F) until risen and crisp (do not open the door during this time). Reduce heat and move to a cooler part of the oven until éclairs are light and dry inside, about 30 min. altogether. Place on a cooling tray, and slit open. When cold, fill the cavities with stiffly whipped, sweetened cream flavored with vanilla. Spread tops with Chocolate or Coffee Glacé Icing. Put the icing on in a straight line, using a teaspoon — hold the éclair in a slanting position when doing so.

9-10 éclairs   Cooking time – 30 min.

FRUIT FLAN

Pâte Sucrée, using 1 cup flour, etc.

Filling:

1 medium-sized can of fruit *or* ¾ lb. fresh fruit, e.g. strawberries, pears, pineapple, cherries, apricots, peaches, etc.

Coating Glaze:

⅝ cup syrup from canned fruit, *or* fruit juice *or* water	Sugar (if necessary) 1 tsp. arrowroot Lemon juice to taste

For Decoration:

Whipped sweetened cream

Line a 7-in. flan ring with the pastry. Prick the bottom of the flan, and bake it "blind." Bake for about 30 min. first in a fairly hot oven (200 °C, 400 °F) reducing the heat to moderate (180 °C, 350 °F) as the pastry sets. When the pastry is cooked, remove the paper and pebbles or beans used for blind baking and replace the shell in the oven for 5 min. to dry the bottom. Allow to cool.

If fresh fruit is used, stew gently until tender, if necessary. Drain the fruit. Place the sugar, if used, and liquid in a pan and boil for 10 min. Blend the arrowroot with some

lemon juice and add it to the syrup, stirring all the time. Continue stirring, cook for 3 min., then cool slightly. Arrange fruit attractively in the flan shell and coat it with fruit syrup. Then flan can be decorated with piped whipped, sweetened cream.

FRUIT TARTLETS

Pâte sucrée *or* shortcrust pastry, using 1 cup flour, etc.

Filling:

Fresh *or* canned fruit, chopped e.g. apples, pears, cherries, peaches, raspberries, strawberries

Coating Glaze:

1 tsp. arrowroot ⅝ cup fruit syrup *or* flavored stock syrup	A few drops of food coloring

Decoration:

3 cups sweetened whipped cream *or* meringue

Roll out the pastry, cut out with a fluted cutter and line small tartlet tins. Bake "blind" in a fairly hot oven (220 °C, 425 °F) for 10-15 min. Remove weighted paper and return tartlets to the oven to dry. Allow to cool. When cool, arrange drained fruit neatly in the shells. Blend the arrowroot with a little syrup, boil the remaining syrup, and gently stir in the blended mixture. Cook over low heat until thickening, stirring very gently so that air bubbles do not form. Pour the glaze over the fruit, and allow to get quite cold. Top with either piped cream or meringue. In the latter case, place the tartlets briefly in a very cool oven (145°C, 290°F) to brown the top of the meringue slightly.

8-10 tartlets

STOCK SYRUP

4 cups sugar	2½ cups water

Dissolve the sugar in the water by heating

78

gently below boiling point. Stir, scraping the pan bottom to prevent the sugar settling before dissolving. When melted, raise the heat and boil 220 °F, skimming while boiling. Strain, cool slightly, and pour into heated jars. Cover with paper, but do not cover tightly.

This syrup will keep for some time. You can dilute it to a thin syrup, or to work fondant, coat fruit, make water ices and ice cream, and many other purposes.

GOOSEBERRY TART

Shortcrust pastry, using 1½ cups flour, etc. 4½ cups gooseberries	2 tbs. water ½ cup brown sugar

Top and tail the gooseberries with a pair of scissors; wash the gooseberries well. Place ½ of them in an 8 in. pie dish; add the sugar and water and then the remaining gooseberries, piling them high in the center. Line the edge of the dish with pastry; cover with the remaining pastry. Bake in a fairly hot oven (200 °C, 400 °F), reducing the heat to moderate (180 °C, 350 °F) when the pastry is set. Continue cooking until the fruit is tender — about 45 min. altogether. Dredge with sugar and serve.

6 servings

LEMON MERINGUE PIE

Shortcrust pastry, using 1 cup flour, etc. ¼ cup cornstarch Rind and juice of 2 lemons	2-4 tbs. granulated sugar 2 tbs. butter 2 eggs ⅜ cup sugar

Line a 7-in. flan ring the pastry and bake it "blind." Make the lemon juice up to 1¼ cups with water. Blend the cornstarch in a little of the lemon liquid, boil the remaining liquid, and pour it over the blended cornstarch, stirring all the time. Put the mixture back in the pan, boil for 3 min., and add the granulated sugar, grated lemon rind, and butter. Allow to cool slightly, add the egg yolks, and pour the mixture into the flan shell. Bake in a moderate oven (180 °C, 350 °F) until set. Beat the egg whites stiffly, fold in the sugar, and pile on top of the flan. Dredge with sugar and return to the oven (140 °C, 290 °F) until the meringue is set and lightly browned.

6 servings   Cooking time – 45-50 min.

RED CURRANT AND RASPBERRY TART

Shortcrust pastry, using 1½ cups flour, etc.	4½ cups red currants 1½ cups raspberries 2-3 tbs. sugar

Strip the currants from the stalks, rinse, and place ½ of the currants in an 8-in. pie dish. Add the sugar, hulled raspberries, then the remaining red currants, piling them high in the center. Line the edge of the dish with pastry. Cover with pastry, brush lightly with water, and dredge well with sugar. Bake in a fairly hot oven (200 °C, 400 °F) for about ¾ hr.

6 servings   Cooking time – about 45 min.

RHUBARB TART

Shortcrust pastry, using 1½ cups flour, etc.	1½ lb. rhubarb ½ cup sugar

Wipe the rhubarb, remove the skin, if it is coarse, and cut into 1-in. lengths. Make like an Apple Tart.

6 servings   Cooking time – 45 min.

VANILLA SLICES

Puff pastry, using ¾ cup flour, etc.	A little glacé icing

Filling:

1¼ cups milk 3 tbs. cornstarch 2 egg yolks *or* 1 whole egg	2 tbs. sugar ½ tsp. vanilla extract

Roll pastry ½ in. thick and cut into fingers 4 by 1 in. Bake in a fairly hot oven (220 °C,

Fruit tartlets before decorating

retards its growth and too much heat kills it.

Once yeast has started raising a dough, cover the bowl containing the dough with a damp cloth to prevent the surface drying out. Do not raise the dough for too long, or it will become overstretched and collapse. Always give it a chance to rise a second time to replace the air knocked out when kneading it after its first rising. Most yeast doughs should be baked in a hot oven to kill the yeast cells.

BABAS WITH RUM SYRUP

2 cups flour	¼ cup milk
Pinch of salt	4 eggs
½ oz. yeast	½ cup butter
2 tbs. sugar	⅜ cup currants

Rum Syrup:

⅜ cup sugar	½ cup rum
⅝ cup water	½ cup sherry
Rind of ½ lemon	

Grease 9 dariole or baba molds.

Sift the flour and salt into a warm bowl. Cream the yeast with a pinch of sugar and add to it the warm milk. Mix this into the flour to form a soft dough. Beat well until the dough leaves the sides of the bowl clean. Cover the bowl with a damp cloth and leave the dough to rise in a warm (but not hot) place until about twice its size. When the dough has risen sufficiently, add 2 eggs, the melted butter, and 2 tbs. sugar; beat in well. Then add the rest of the eggs and the currants and beat again for 5-10 min., until the dough is smooth and glossy. Half-fill the molds with the mixture. Put them in a warm place until the mixture has risen to the top of the molds. Bake in a fairly hot oven (220 °C, 425 °F) for about 20-25 min., until brown and firm.

Put the ⅜ cup sugar and water into a pan with the thinly peeled lemon rind.
Boil for 10 min.; add the rum sherry; strain.

Reheat the syrup. Soak the babas in it for a minute; lift them out and serve immediately, with the syrup poured around.

425 °F) until pastry is well risen. Allow to cool.

Blend the cornstarch with the milk, beat in the egg yolks and sugar, and cook over a gentle heat until thick. Beat in the vanilla. Allow to cool.

Slit carefully through the center of the pastry fingers, spread the custard over 1 half and sandwich the halves together again. Spread tops thinly with glacé icing.

8 slices   Cooking time – 20 min.

YEAST MIXTURES

Some desserts and cakes are made with a yeast dough. In making these, remember that yeast is a plant and needs gentle heat, moisture, and food to make it grow. Cold

Fruit tartlets with meringue topping

VARIATION

Babas with kirsch Make a syrup by boiling together ¾ cup granulated sugar, 1 cup water, and the thinly peeled rind of ½ lemon. Strain, when thick, and cool a little. Add the kirsch. Soak the babas in the syrup for 1 min. just before serving.

9 babas

MARIGNONS

Make like pomponettes, but use boat-shaped molds instead of tartlet molds.

POMPONETTES OR
BABY SAVARINS

Savarin mixture as below	Rum sauce mixture as below

Decoration:

Apricot Glaze	Sweetened
Glacé cherries	whipped cream

Half-fill lightly greased deep fluted tartlet molds with savarin mixture, let rise, and cook like a large savarin. Soak in rum sauce. Make a slit or split in each pomponette. Glaze all over. Finish with a decoration of whipped cream piped into the split, and a slice of glacé cherry.

PUDDING A L'AMBASSADRICE

Savarin mixture cooked in a plain mold.

Custard Filling:

2 tbs. butter	1 egg yolk
¼ cup flour	¼ cup cream
⅝ cup milk	2 tsp. sugar

Caramel:

¼ cup sugar	¼ cup water

Custard:

1 cup milk	1 egg yolk
¼ cup cream	2 tsp. sugar
2 eggs	

Cook the savarin and allow to cool.

Make the custard filling: melt the butter, add the flour, work in the milk, then bring to a boil, stirring well. Add the beaten egg yolk, cream, and sugar; cook gently until the mixture thickens. Let cool.

Heat a soufflé dish and have ready a thickly folded band of newspaper to encircle the dish so that it can be held firmly in one hand. Prepare the caramel by heating together the sugar and water, stir until it boils, then remove the spoon and allow to boil without stirring until it is golden brown. Pour the caramel into the warm soufflé dish and twist around until the sides and bowl are well-coated with caramel.

Slice the savarin, spread it with the custard filling, and pile it into the soufflé dish.

Make the custard: warm the milk and cream and pour it on the 2 beaten eggs and egg yolk; add the sugar. Strain over the savarin mixture; cover. Steam very gently for about 45 min., until firm.

SAVARIN

1 cup flour	1 egg
Pinch of salt	½ tbs. sugar
1 tbs. yeast	3 tbs. butter
2½ tbs. warm water	

Rum Sauce:

⅜ cup sugar	1-2 tbs. rum
⅝ cup water	Juice of ½ lemon

Decoration:

Apricot jam
Blanched almonds, browned

Sift the flour and salt into a bowl and let warm. Cream the yeast with the tepid water. Make a well in the center of the flour and pour in the yeast mixture. Sprinkle over the top with a little of the flour from the side of the bowl. Let rise for 10-15 min. in a warm place. Add the egg gradually, beating well to a smooth elastic dough, using a little more tepid water if necessary. Knead well. Put the dough back into the bowl and press down, sprinkle the sugar on the top, and put on the butter in small pieces. Cover with a damp cloth and leave in a warm place to double its size. Beat well again until all the sugar and butter are absorbed. Grease a border mold and fill it ⅓ of the way up with the mixture. Let rise in a warm place until the mixture just reaches the top of the mold. Then bake in a fairly hot oven (200 °C, 400 °F) for about 20 min.

Make the sauce: boil the water and sugar steadily for about 10 min. Add the rum and lemon juice.

Turn the savarin out onto a hot dish, prick with a needle or hat pin, and soak well in the sauce. Coat with hot sieved apricot jam and decorate with spikes of almonds, etc. Serve with the rest of the sauce poured around.

4 servings

Ices and Iced Drinks

We mostly use two kinds of ices: water ices and ice creams.

Water Ices and Sherbets

Water ices are made from the juice of fresh fruit or fruit puree mixed with syrup or fruit syrup. Sherbets are half-frozen water ices containing egg white or gelatin. At formal banquets they are served in sherbet cups or glasses immediately before the roast to clear the palate, but at more informal meals they are often served as a sweet course.

Ice Creams

These are sometimes made almost entirely of cream — sweetened, flavored, and decorated in many ways. More frequently the so-called "ice cream" consists principally of custard of varying degrees of richness, with the addition of fruit pulp, almonds, chocolate, coffee, liqueurs, and other flavorings. The cream, when used, should be heavy cream; evaporated milk can be subsituted for part or all of the cream, but the can should first be boiled, unopened, for 20 min., then cooled quickly and, if possible, chilled for 24 hr. in a refrigerator.

To obtain a smooth, even-textured ice cream in a refrigerator, the mixture must be frozen quickly and beaten well. The quicker the freezing, the less likelihood there is of ice crystals forming, so set the refrigerator to the coldest point ½ hr. before putting

White Coffee and Chocolate Ice Cream Bombe   Apricot Ice Cream

the mixture to freeze, unless instructed otherwise in the recipe. Chill all ingredients and utensils before use.

Prepare the mixture, place it in an ice tray, and replace the tray in the freezing compartment.

Air acts as a deterrent to crystal formation, so remove the mixture after ½ hr. and beat well in a chilled bowl. Replace in the tray and put back into the freezing compartment.

Ice Cream Mousses
Besides custard and cream ices, you can make a lighter iced mixture for use in molded ice cream desserts, such as bombes, made in round molds. The mixture is uncooked and is made with cream, sweetened condensed milk, and whipped egg whites, well-flavored. The bombe is coated with a more solid custard and cream iced mixture and is filled with the mousse mixture.

Molding bombes or other shapes in ice cream

Partly fill the moistened mold with a custard and cream iced mixture. In the center place a smaller bowl than the mold itself, and weight it with dried beans or what you find convenient. The ice cream mixture surrounding it should reach the top of the mold through being displaced, but should not trickle into the inner bowl.

Cover the mold tightly (e.g. with foil) and freeze. When firmly frozen, remove from the freezer, and fill the inner bowl with hot water. Twist it to remove it from the surrounding ice cream. Fill the hole thus left with ice cream mousse mixture. Re-freeze.

To dislodge, or unmold, the dessert, dip the mold very quickly, to the brim, in hot water. Invert onto a moist plate immediately, and jerk sharply to dislodge the contents. Freeze again briefly to harden the outside. Remove from the freezer in time for the ice cream to soften slightly before serving, and decorate at this stage.

SYRUP FOR WATER ICES

1-4 cups sugar	2½ cups water

Place the sugar and water in a heavy saucepan. Allow the sugar to dissolve over low heat, without stirring. When dissolved, boil the mixture gently for 10 min., or, if you have a candy thermometer, until it registers 220 °F. Skim to remove scum. Strain, cool, and store.

CIDER ICE

1 large cooking apple	1¼ cups syrup
1¼ cups cider	Juice of 1 large lemon

Peel, core, and slice the apple. Cook in a covered saucepan with 1 tbs. of water. Pass the cooked apple through a fine hair *or* nylon sieve and add all other ingredients. Chill and freeze.

6 servings   Time – 2-2½ hr.

LEMON WATER ICE

6 lemons	3¾ cups syrup
2 oranges	

Thinly peel the fruit and place the rind in a basin. Add the hot syrup, cover, and cool. Add the juice of the lemons and oranges. Strain, chill, and freeze.

6 servings   Time – 1½ hr.

PINEAPPLE WATER ICE

1¼ cups canned pineapple juice	2 tbs. lemon juice
2½ cups syrup	

Thoroughly mix all ingredients. Chill and freeze.

6 servings   Time – 1½-2 hr.

RASPBERRY or STRAWBERRY WATER ICE

3 cups ripe strawberries *or* raspberries	Juice of 2 lemons 2½ cups syrup

Rub the fruit through a nylon sieve and add the lemon juice. Add the syrup and a little coloring if necessary. Chill and freeze.

6 servings   Time – 1 hr.

LEMON SHERBET

2½ cups water 1 cup sugar	1¼ cups lemon juice 2 egg whites

Dissolve the sugar in the water. Boil it for 10 min., strain, and cool. Add the lemon juice and the stiffly beaten egg whites. Freeze, and serve at once.

6 servings   Time – 1½ hr.

PINEAPPLE SHERBET

2½ cups water 1 cup sugar	1¼ cups canned pineapple juice 2 egg whites

Dissolve the sugar in the water. Boil it for 10 min.; strain, and cool. Add the pineapple juice and the stiffly beaten egg whites. Freeze, and serve at once.

6 servings   Time – 1½ hr.

ICE CREAM CUSTARDS
Economical

¼ cup cornstarch 2½ cups milk	½ cup sugar

Blend the cornstarch with a little of the milk. Boil remaining milk and pour onto the blended mixture. Return to pan and simmer, stirring continuously. Add sugar, cover, and allow to cool.

Rich

2½ cups milk 3-8 eggs	½ cup sugar

Heat the milk. Beat together eggs and sugar. Add the hot milk, stirring constantly. Return to pan and cook without boiling until custard coats the back of a wooden spoon. Strain, cover, and cool.

Very Rich

8 egg yolks ½ cup sugar	2½ cups cream Flavoring

Cream yolks and sugar together until very thick. Place cream in a saucepan and bring to boil. Pour boiling cream over yolks and sugar, stirring well. Return to pan and stir over heat until it thickens without boiling. Strain, add vanilla or other flavoring, and use as required.

APRICOT ICE CREAM

Make like Black Currant Ice Cream, using apricots and yellow coloring instead of black currants and red coloring.

BANANA ICE CREAM

3 bananas 2 tbs. lemon juice	1¼ cups cream *or* ⅝ cup cream and ⅝ cup custard ¼-½ cup sugar

Peel and slice the bananas; cover with lemon juice. Pass fruit through a nylon sieve. Add the half-whipped cream, cold custard, if used, and sugar. Chill and freeze.

6 servings

BLACK CURRANT ICE CREAM

1½ cups ripe black currants ⅜ cup sugar ⅝ cup water Rind and juice of 1 lemon	Few drops of red food coloring 1¼ cups custard ⅝ cup cream

Place black currants, sugar, and water, peel and strained juice of lemon, and a few drops of carmine in a pan and allow to just boil. Pass through a nylon sieve. Add the custard, and partly freeze. Add the whipped and sweetened cream and finish freezing.

6 servings   Time – 2½ hr.

Banana Split

Coupe Jacque

BURNT ALMOND ICE CREAM

3/8 cup almonds	**1 qt. custard**
1/4 cup sugar	**1 tbs. kirsch (optional)**
1/2 cup cream	

Blanch, shred, and bake the almonds until brown. Put the sugar and a few drops of water in a saucepan and boil until it acquires a deep golden color. Add the cream, boil, and stir into the custard. Chill, add almonds and kirsch, if used, then freeze the mixture.

6-7 servings Time – 2 1/2-3 hr.

CARAMEL ICE CREAM

1/4 cup sugar	**1 qt. custard**
1/2 cup cream	

Put the sugar into a small saucepan with a few drops of water and boil until a deep golden color. Add the cream and, when boiling, stir into the custard. Chill and freeze.

6-7 servings Time – 1 1/2-2 hr.

CHOCOLATE ICE CREAM

4 oz. plain chocolate	**5/8 cup cream**
1/4 cup water	**1-2 tsp. vanilla extract**
1 1/4 cups custard	

Break chocolate in pieces; place in pan; add water. Dissolve over low heat. Add melted chocolate to the custard. Cool. Add the half-whipped cream and vanilla to taste. Chill and freeze.

6-8 servings

COFFEE ICE CREAM

3 tbs. instant coffee	**1 1/4 cups cream**
1/4 cup hot water	**3/8 cup sugar**

Dissolve the coffee in the hot water. Cool. Half-whip the cream and add sugar. Fold in the dissolved coffee. Chill and freeze.

6 servings Time – 2 1/2 hr.

GINGER ICE CREAM

1 tsp. ground ginger	**1 1/4 cups cream**
1/4 cup ginger syrup	**5/8 cup custard**
3 oz. chopped preserved ginger	**1/4 cup sugar**

Dissolve the ground ginger in the syrup. Cut the preserved ginger into diced pieces. Half-whip the cream and add to it the custard, ginger, syrup, and sugar. Chill and freeze.

6 servings Time – 2 hr.

MARSHMALLOW ICE CREAM

14 marshmallows	**5/8 cup fruit puree**
5/8 cup evaporated milk	**3/8 cup sugar**
	5/8 cup cream

Melt the marshmallows in the evaporated milk over hot water. Cool. Add the fruit puree and sugar. Lastly, fold in the half-whipped cream. Pour into the tray and freeze at medium temperature. Stir once after the first 1/2 hr. and continue to freeze for another 1 1/2 hr.

6 servings

ORANGE ICE CREAM

3 oranges	**Saffron yellow coloring**
1/4 cup sugar	**Red coloring**
1 qt. custard	

Remove the outer, yellow skin of the oranges by rubbing them with lumps of sugar. Dissolve the sugar in 1 tbs. of hot water. Mix with the strained juice of oranges. Stir into the custard and add the colorings until of the desired shade. Chill and freeze.

6-8 servings Time – 45 min.

PISTACHIO ICE CREAM

1 qt. custard	**Orange-flower water**
1 cup pistachio nuts	**1 tbs. noyeau**
	Green coloring

Blanch the nuts and remove the skins. Pound the nuts, gradually adding a little orange-flower water. Add the noyeau and coloring to the cold custard. Chill and freeze; when partially frozen, add the nuts.

6-8 servings   Time – 1-1¼ hr.

RASPBERRY ICE CREAM

1 8-oz. pkg. raspberries	⅝ cup custard
⅝ cups cream	¼ cup sugar

Drain the raspberries and pass through a nylon sieve. (Puree and juice together should measure 1¼ cups.) Mix with custard, then add the half-whipped cream. Add the sugar, and a little coloring, if necessary. Chill and freeze.

6 servings

STRAWBERRY ICE CREAM

⅝ cup milk	2 tsp. sugar
1¼ cups cream	1 tsp. lemon juice
1-2 egg yolks	
¾ cup sugar	Red coloring
3 cups strawberries	

Put milk and cream in a saucepan and bring nearly to boiling point. Beat together the egg yolks and ¾ cup sugar, add to the milk and cream, and stir over a low heat until they thicken. Pass the strawberries through a sieve, together with the 2 tsp. sugar. Mix with the custard, add the lemon juice and red to color. Chill and freeze.

6-8 servings   Time – about 1-1½ hr.

TEA ICE CREAM

2½ cups custard	¼ cup cream
1¼ cups strong tea	¼ cup sugar

Strain the tea, add the sugar, and let it cool. Mix all ingredients together. Chill and freeze.

6-8 servings   Time – 35-40 min.

VANILLA ICE CREAM

⅝ cup cream	1 tbs. sugar
1¼ cups cold custard	1 tsp. vanilla extract

Half-whip the cream. Add the custard, sugar, and vanilla. Chill and freeze.

VANILLA ICE CREAM (Rich)

1¼ cups cream	1 tsp. vanilla
1¼ cups cold custard	¼ cup sugar

Half-whip the cream. Add the custard, vanilla, and sugar. Chill and freeze.

WALNUT ICE CREAM

¾ cup walnuts	Vanilla extract
Orange-flower water	1 qt. custard

Chop the nuts, gradually adding a little orange-flower water. Add the vanilla extract to the custard. Chill and freeze; when partially frozen, add the walnuts.

6-8 servings   Time – 1-1¼ hr.

WHITE COFFEE ICE CREAM

2 cups fresh roasted coffee beans	2½ cups cream *or* milk

Place the beans and the cream *or* milk in saucepan and heat for an hour but do not let them boil. Strain. Use this mixture to make one of the basic custards and then finish as for Vanilla Ice Cream.

FAMILY DESSERTS WITH PURCHASED ICE CREAM

While homemade ice cream is delicious, decorated fancy ice cream dishes are often best made with purchased ice cream, which is light yet firm and is a healthful food. For family use especially it is both labor-saving and inexpensive.

BANANA SPLIT

6 bananas	¾ cups sweetened
1 pt. vanilla	whipped cream
ice cream	½ cup chopped
1¼ cups Melba	walnuts
Sauce	8 maraschino
	cherries

Peel bananas, split in half lengthwise, and place in small oval dishes. Place 2 small scoops or slices of ice cream between the halves of bananas. Coat the ice cream with Melba Sauce; sprinkle with chopped nuts. Decorate with whipped cream and cherries.

CHOCOLATE SUNDAE

½ pt. chocolate	½ cup chopped
ice cream	walnuts
1¼ cups chocolate	¾ cup sweetened
sauce	whipped cream
½ pt. vanilla	8 maraschino
ice cream	cherries

Place a scoop of chocolate ice cream in 6-8 sundae glasses; coat with chocolate sauce. Place a scoop of vanilla ice cream on top; coat with chocolate sauce. Sprinkle with nuts. Decorate with whipped cream and cherries.

COUPE JACQUES

1 pt. vanilla	1 banana
ice cream	1 peach
1 pt. strawberry	¼ cup raspberries
ice cream	¾ cup sweetened
⅓ cup peeled	whipped cream
grapes	

Place 1 portion of vanilla ice cream and 1 portion of strawberry ice cream in a deep dish. Chop and mix the fruit and place over the ice cream. Garnish with whipped cream.

6-8 servings

GRAPEFRUIT BASKETS

3 grapefruits	1 11-oz. can
2 oranges,	mandarin
segmented	oranges,
1 qt. orange	drained
sherbet	6 maraschino
	cherries

Cut the grapefruit in half, making a decorative serrated edge. Scoop out the flesh carefully and remove the pith from each segment. Toss with the orange segments and mandarin oranges. Place scoops of ice cream in each grapefruit shell and arrange the fruit around. Decorate with a maraschino cherry and serve in individual dishes.

6 servings

KNICKERBOCKER GLORY

2½ cups red	2½ cups Melba
gelatin dessert	Sauce
2½ cups yellow	½ cup chopped
gelatin dessert	walnuts
1 8-oz. can chopped	¾ cup sweetened
peaches	whipped cream
1 9-oz. can	8 maraschino
pineapple	cherries
1 qt. vanilla	
ice cream	

Make the gelatin desserts, allow to set, then whip with a fork. Place small portions of chopped fruit in the bottom of tall sundae glasses. Cover these with 1 tbs. of whipped gelatin. Place a scoop or slice of ice cream on top of the gelatin. Coat the ice cream with Melba Sauce. Repeat again with fruit, gelatin ice cream, and sauce. Sprinkle with chopped nuts. Top with sweetened whipped cream. Place a cherry on top of each.

6 individual glasses

MERINGUE GLACÉ CHANTILLY

1 qt. vanilla	¾ cup sweetened
ice cream *or*	whipped cream
16 meringue	8 maraschino
cases	cherries

Place a scoop or slice of ice cream in 8 small oval dishes. Set a meringue case on either side of the ice cream. Pipe a large rose of cream on top of the ice cream. Place a cherry on top.

8 individual dishes

OMELETTE SOUFFLÉE EN SURPRISE

1 round Genoese Pastry *or* sponge cake	3 egg whites A few drops of vanilla extract
1 tbs. liqueur 1 egg yolk ¼ cup sugar	1 creamed rice pudding *or* 1 pt. vanilla ice cream

Decoration:

Glacé cherries	Angelica

Place the cake on a silver or ovenproof dish and soak with liqueur. Whip the egg yolk and sugar until thick, and fold in the stiffly beaten egg whites. Add vanilla extract and place the soufflé mixture in a pastry bag with a large rose pipe. Place the ice cream on top of the cake. Completely

Grapefruit Baskets

Knickerbocker Glory

Orange and Ginger Milk Shake

93

cover with piped soufflé mixture. Dredge with confectioners' sugar and place in a very hot oven for 3 min. Decorate, and serve immediately.

6-8 servings

PEACH MELBA

4-5 firm, ripe peaches	½ cup sugar
¼ cup Melba Sauce	1 pt. vanilla ice cream,
Vanilla extract	homemade *or* purchased

Halve and peel the peaches. Add the vanilla to the syrup and dissolve the sugar in it. Poach the peaches in the syrup until tender but not broken. Lift out the peaches, drain them on a sieve, and allow to get thoroughly cold. Serve them piled around a mound of vanilla ice cream in a silver dish. Set this dish in another dish containing shaved ice. Pour over a rich raspberry syrup, which must be previously iced. Serve at once.

This is the original recipe created in honour of Dame Nellie Melba. It is now often made as follows:

1 pt. vanilla ice cream	1¼ cups Melba Sauce
6 canned peach halves	¾ cup sweetened whipped cream

Place a scoop or slice of ice cream in 6 sundae glasses. Cover with a peach half. Coat with Melba Sauce. Pipe a large rose of cream on top of each.

Other fruits are also used. Pears dipped in lemon juice team well with raspberries, for instance.

6 individual glasses

STRAWBERRY LAYER GÂTEAU

1 pt. vanilla ice cream	¾ cup sweetened whipped cream
1½ cups strawberries	Sugar

Cut the ice cream, which must be firm, in ½ horizontally. Cover the lower ½ with halves of strawberries. Sprinkle with sugar and replace the top half. Pipe with rosettes of cream and place small straw-

berries all over the top. Dredge with sugar and serve immediately.

6 servings

SWISS CHOCOLATE LOG

1 chocolate Swiss roll	¾ cup sweetened whipped cream
1 pt. ice cream	

Cut the Swiss roll into 7 slices and the ice cream into 6. Arrange on a long dish by sandwiching alternate slices of Swiss roll and ice cream pressed together. Pipe the whipped cream on top of the ice cream and dredge the Swiss roll with confectioners' sugar.

6 servings

CHOCOLATE SAUCE FOR ICE CREAM

2 rounded tsp. cornstarch	6 round tsp. sugar
4 rounded tsp. cocoa	1¼ cups water
1 tbs. butter	3 drops vanilla extract

Blend together the cornstarch, cocoa, and sugar with a little of the water. Boil remaining water and pour onto blended mixture. Return to pan and boil for 2 min., stirring constantly. Add vanilla and butter. Serve hot or cold.

COFFEE SAUCE FOR ICE CREAM

6 tbs. freshly ground coffee	¾ tbs. gelatin
	3 egg yolks
1 pt. water	⅜ cup sugar

Boil the water and pour over the coffee. Strain when cool. Dissolve the gelatin in 1 tbs. water. Beat together the egg yolks and sugar. Place all ingredients in a saucepan. Cook slowly, without boiling, until the mixture thickens. Strain and chill. Use as required.

MELBA SAUCE

To make Melba Sauce, pass the required quantity of fresh or frozen raspberries through a nylon sieve and sweeten with confectioners' sugar. The sauce is not cooked. Use as required.

ICED COFFEE

1¼ cups milk	A few drops of
¾ cup sugar	vanilla extract
5 cups strong,	1¼ cups cream
clear, hot coffee	

Place the milk and sugar in a saucepan. Bring almost to a boil; add the coffee and vanilla extract, allow to cool. Strain, stir in the cream, and chill until it has the consistency of thick cream. Serve very cold in tall glasses, and pass sugar separately.

ICE CREAM BRANDY PUNCH

2½ cups milk	1 pt. vanilla
1 egg	ice cream
½ cup brandy	

Place the milk, brandy, and egg in a bowl. Beat well. Add the ice cream cut in small pieces. Beat until frothy. Pour into a punch bowl and serve immediately.

6-8 glasses

MILK PUNCH

5 cups milk	2 tbs. brandy
½ cup sugar	*or* rum
	¾ cup cream

Boil the milk; dissolve the sugar in it; strain and chill. Add the brandy *or* rum and the whipped cream. Mix well and half-freeze. Serve in a half-frozen condition in small china sherbet cups and, if liked, grate a little nutmeg or cinnamon on top before serving.

6-8 servings

ORANGE AND GINGER MILK SHAKE

2 pts. vanilla	6 pieces of stem
ice cream	ginger
1 pint milk	1 tbs. sugar
Rind and juice	Julienne strips of
of 2 oranges	orange peel

Soften 1½ packs of the ice cream and blend together with the milk, orange rind and juice, ginger, and sugar until smooth. Pour into chilled glasses. Decorate with the remainder of the ice cream cut into wedges; garnish with orange strips.

Hot and Cool Drinks

COCOA, TO MAKE

Allow 1½ tsp. cocoa to ⅝ cup milk and ⅝ cup water. Mix the cocoa smoothly with a little water. Boil the rest of the water and milk, and pour onto the cocoa, stirring well. Sweeten to suit your taste.

COFFEE, TO MAKE

To make perfect coffee, the beans should be roasted, or at least ground, just before using them. When this is not practicable, store home or shop-ground coffee in an airtight jar.

Method I Warm an ordinary china jug, put in the coarsely ground coffee, pour the boiling water onto it, and stir vigorously. Allow the jug to stand for 1 min., then skim off any floating coffee grains; stand for another 4 min., closely covered, where the contents will remain just below boiling point. The coffee can then be poured slowly or strained into another warmed china jug and used at once.

Method 2 Put the coffee (coarsely ground) with the water into an enamel saucepan and bring almost to a boil. Reduce the heat and simmer very gently for 3 min. Dash in 1 tsp. cold water to help the grounds to settle. Strain into a warmed coffeepot or jug.

Method 3 Use a percolator and fine- or medium-ground coffee. Put into the percolator as much fresh cold water as is required, and bring to a boil. Put the coffee into the basket and insert it in the percolator; cover, and return to heat. Allow to percolate *gently* 6-8 min.

Method 4 (Cafe filter) Heat a coffeepot or individual cups, place the finely ground coffee in the strainer over the coffeepot, and slowly pour over freshly boiled water and allow to drip through. When the water has dripped through, remove strainer — if the coffee is not strong enough, filter again.

Coffee may be served black *(Café Noir)*, with milk *(Café au Lait)*, or with cream *(Café Crème)*. When serving *Café au Lait,* it is usual to pour the 2 liquids into the cup at the same time; *the milk should be hot but not boiled.*

Liqueurs such as kirsch, cognac, liqueur brandy, or some other sweet liqueur are usually served with coffee.

TEA, TO MAKE

To make good tea, it is necessary that the water be boiling, and freshly boiled. It is a best to empty the kettle and refill it with fresh cold water, and make the tea the moment the water boils.

The teapot should be thoroughly warmed before making the tea. The boiling water should be poured on the tea, then allowed to stand 3-4 min.; it should never stand longer. Some people like to stir the tea before pouring it out.

BISHOP

1 large orange	1 bottle of port
12 cloves	Sugar

Stick the cloves into the orange, put it into a closely covered ovenproof bowl, put into the oven, and roast until nice and brown. Cut it up into 8 pieces and remove the seeds. Put the port wine into a clean saucepan with the pieces of orange, and heat gently. Sweeten to taste with sugar and simmer for 20 min., but be careful not to let it boil. Strain off the liquid through a fine sieve and serve at once — hot.

HOT PUNCH (1)

1 large lemon	Pinch of cloves
¼-½ cup sugar	1¼ cups brandy
Pinch of ground	1¼ cups rum
cinnamon	2½ cups boiling
Pinch of grated	water
nutmeg	

Remove the rind of the lemon by rubbing it with some of the sugar. Put all the sugar, the cinnamon, nutmeg, cloves, brandy, rum, and boiling water into a stewpan; heat gently on the side of the stove, but do not let it boil. Strain the lemon juice into a punch bowl; add the hot liquid; serve at once.

HOT PUNCH (2)

5 cups ale	Sugar to taste
2½ cups boiling	Pinch of ground
water	cinnamon
¾ cup rum	Pinch of ground
¾ cup whisky	cloves
¾ cup gin	Pinch of grated
1 lemon, thinly	nutmeg
sliced	

Put all ingredients into a large stewpan and bring nearly to boiling point. Strain into a punch bowl, add a few fresh thin slices of lemon, and serve.

CHAMPAGNE CUP

1 bottle of	½ tsp. maraschino
champagne	juice
2 bottles of	1 liqueur glass
soda water	brandy
A few strips of	1 tsp. sugar
lemon rind	(optional)

Chill the champagne and soda water for 1 hr. When ready to serve, put the strips of lemon rind into a large glass jug, add the maraschino and brandy, pour in the champagne and soda water; serve at once. If sugar is added, it should be stirred in gradually.

CIDER CUP

1 bottle of cider	A few thin strips
1 bottle of	of lemon rind
soda water	(without pith)
1 liqueur glass	2 tsp. lemon
brandy	juice
A few thin strips	3 tsp. sugar
cucumber rind	*or* to taste

Chill the cider and soda water for ½ hr. Put the brandy, cucumber and lemon rind, lemon juice, and sugar into a large jug; add the chilled cider and soda water. Serve at once.

FRUIT PUNCH

4-5 large fleshy	1 large can of
cooking apples	pears (only a
¾ cup sugar	little fruit is
2½ cups water	required)
2 lemons	A few cherries
	5 cups ginger
	beer

Peel and core the apples and cut up small. Simmer with the sugar, water and lemon rinds for 15 min. in a covered saucepan. Strain through muslin and allow the liquid to cool. Add to this the liquid from pears and the juice of the lemons. Stone a few cherries, spear on cocktail sticks, and put them in the glasses. Dice a little of the pears and put a few pieces in each glass, with some thinly peeled pieces of lemon rind, if liked. Add the ginger beer to the pear and apple juice mixture and serve in the glasses.

Gâteaux for Desserts and Parties

Today, we use gâteaux more and more as our party desserts, as well as for children's and other tea parties. Here is a selection you can serve with pride, mostly based on Genoese and other pastry.

GENOESE PASTRY

This pastry is used as a base for desserts and as a basic mixture for small iced cakes and gâteaux of various kinds.

1 cup flour	½ cup sugar
Pinch of salt	6 tbs. butter *or*
4 eggs	margarine

Sift flour and salt. Beat eggs and sugar in a bowl over a pan of hot water until thick. Clarify the fat and fold lightly into egg mixture, then fold in salted flour. Pour into lined Swiss roll pan and bake in a moderate oven (180 °C, 350 °F). When cold (after 24 hr.), cut and use as desired for small iced cakes, etc.

Cooking time – 30-40 min.

APRICOT GÂTEAU

1 round of	2 tbs. sieved
Genoese Pastry,	apricot jam
6 in. diameter	
and 1 in. thick	

2 tbs. sherry	1 in. width
or fruit juice	ribbon to tie
2 doz. Sponge	around the sponge
Finger biscuits	fingers (about 12 in.)

Filling:

1 15-oz. can	1 pt. heavy
apricots	cream
½ pkg. lemon	Sugar to taste
gelatin	

Decoration:

Angelica

Place the round of cake on a serving plate and sprinkle with the sherry or juice. Trim the Sponge Fingers so that all sides are straight and equal in length, with 1 end trimmed straight across. Melt the gelatin powder in ¾ cup hot apricot juice and allow to cool but not set. Brush inside of trimmed end of each Sponge Finger to 1

Sweetmeats served as Petits Fours in a meringue basket

Pear and ginger sponge gâteau

in. deep with sieved apricot jam; dip 1 edge only in cool gelatin, and press firmly against the side of the round of cake. As each finger is so treated, the jellied edge will be in contact with the dry edge of the adjacent finger, and a firm case will be made without the fingers becoming sodden and crumbling. The rounded, sugary surface of the finger faces outward. Tie the ribbon around the finished case so that the Sponge Fingers are held firmly upright, and allow to set.

Filling Drain the apricots well, and reserve 6 halves for decoration. Cut the remainder into quarters. Whip the cream until the fork leaves a trail; sweeten to taste with sugar. Put $\frac{1}{4}$ of the cream into a pastry bag with rose pipe, for decorating (optional). Stir the quartered apricots into the remainder of the cream. Lastly, trickle in $\frac{1}{4}$ cup of the hot liquid gelatin, stirring constantly. Pour immediately into the Sponge Finger case. Arrange the 6 apricot halves (either whole *or* cut as liked) on the top, and pipe cream roses between and around to cover the surface of the cream. Decorate with leaves of angelica.

Variations Use fresh *or* canned strawberries, chopped pineapple, fruit-flavored ice cream, *or* confectioners' custard filling.

MERINGUE BATON

Shortbread:

$\frac{3}{4}$ cup flour	4 tbs. butter *or*
1 tbs. sugar	margarine
	Jam

Meringue:

2 egg whites	$\frac{1}{2}$ cup sugar

Sift the flour; add the sugar; knead it into the fat. Roll out $\frac{1}{4}$ in. thick and cut into fingers 3 by 1 in. Prick well and cook in a moderate oven (180 °C, 350 °F).

Beat egg whites stiffly, and gradually beat in the sugar. Spread biscuits with a very little jam, pipe meringue on top, and dredge with sugar. Finish in a slow oven (150 °C, 310 °F) until meringue is crisp and light fawn-colored.

8 batons   Cooking time – 40 min.

STRAWBERRY SHORTCAKE

2 cups flour	1$\frac{1}{2}$ tbs. ground
$\frac{1}{8}$ tsp. salt	almonds
Pinch of baking	9 tbs. margarine
powder	$\frac{1}{4}$ cup sugar
	1 egg yolk

Filling:

2$\frac{1}{2}$ cups	$\frac{5}{8}$-1$\frac{1}{4}$ cups
strawberries	whipped cream
Sugar to taste	

Sift flour, salt, and baking powder, and mix with the ground almonds. Cream the fat and sugar, and add egg yolk. Work in the flour mixture as for a shortbread cake. Divide into 3 pieces and roll into rounds a good $\frac{1}{4}$ in. thick. Bake in a moderate oven (180 °C, 350 °F) until golden brown, then allow to become cold. Crush strawberries slightly with sugar to taste, and add a little whipped cream. Spread this onto the first round of shortcake, cover with the second round, and so on, finishing with a layer of strawberries. Pipe whipped cream on top and around the edges. Decorate as desired.

1) Self-rising flour can be used, without the baking powder.

2) Pears make a good addition to the strawberries. Slice the peeled pears, poach them, and drain well before using.
Cooking time – 30-40 min.

APPLE SHORTCAKE

Make the cake as above but use apples for the filling. Peel the apples, cut into neat pieces, and stew in sugar syrup — keep some nice pieces for the top. Alternatively, mix some grated raw apple with lemon juice, then with whipped sweetened cream, and use for filling.

Icings and Fillings

FILLINGS FOR GÂTEAU

Butter icings, confectioners' custard and sieved jam are the most usual fillings. Cream is also used for some cakes, but does not "keep" long. Cream can also be used to make custard-based or jam fillings richer.

Any of these fillings can be flavored with a liqueur or extract to suit your choice, or with a little very strong "instant" coffee or melted chocolate. Chopped glacé or candied fruit, chopped or ground nuts, cake crumbs, or desiccated coconut can be added to any basic filling for an alternative flavoring or as thickening.

Good combination flavorings for cake fillings are made by mixing: coffee and chopped walnuts, coffee and vanilla extract, rum and chocolate or coffee, cherry jam and kirsch or brandy.

CREAM AS FILLING AND TOPPING FOR CAKES, GÂTEAUX, MERINGUE, ETC.

Cream tends to sink into the fabric of a cake or pastry and should only be added shortly before serving.

Whipped cream for cake, meringue, or tart fillings should be stiff. It is best to use heavy cream undiluted by milk, egg white, or light cream.

To sweeten whipped cream for fillings Whip the cream until almost stiff. Then sift in a little confectioners' sugar with a pinch of salt. Whip again. Repeat this process until the cream is as sweet as you want it. If you add all the sugar at once, the cream will liquefy and may be difficult to whip stiffly again. Add any flavoring *before* sweetening. Adjust flavoring after sweetening.

MOCK CREAM

2 tbs. cornstarch	2 tbs. sugar
5/8 cup milk	A few drops of
2 tbs. margarine	vanilla extract

Blend the cornstarch with a little of the milk; put the rest of the milk on to boil. Pour the boiling milk onto the blended cornstarch, stirring well. Return mixture to pan, and cook for 2-3 min. Cool. Cream together the margarine and sugar. Gradually beat the cornstarch mixture into the creamed fat a little at a time; beat well. Stir in the vanilla extract.

ALMOND PASTE OR ICING

Almond Paste — often called Almond Icing or Marzipan — is used to cover rich cakes before applying royal or glacé icing. (It is also used alone to decorate cakes such as Simnel Cake and Battenburg Cake.) It is often colored and flavored and then molded into various shapes to be used for cake decoration.

Strawberry Shortcake with pears

1½ cups	Juice of ½ lemon
confectioners'	1-2 egg yolks
sugar and ¾ cup	¾ tsp. orange
granulated sugar	flower water
or 3 cups	(optional)
confectioners'	¾ tsp. vanilla
sugar	extract
2¼ cups ground	
almonds	

Sift the confectioners' sugar into a bowl and mix with the ground almonds and granulated sugar. Add the lemon juice, extracts, and enough egg yolk to bind the ingredients into a pliable but dry paste. Knead thoroughly by hand until smooth.

A whole egg *or* egg whites may be used instead of egg yolks. Egg yolk gives a richer and yellower paste; egg white gives a whiter, more brittle paste. (The yolks can be used for Almond Paste and the whites for Royal Icing.) This quantity of paste is sufficient to cover the top and sides of an 8-in. cake.

For colored Almond Paste, use a few drops of food coloring and egg white rather than yolks.

To apply Almond Paste To cover the top and sides of a rich fruit cake, the cake top should be fairly level and the surface free from loose crumbs.

Brush the top and sides with warm Apricot Glaze, using a pastry brush. Dredge a little sugar onto a clean board and roll out the Almond Paste to a round 4 in. wider than the diameter of the cake. Place the cake in the center of this, with its glazed top downward and work the paste upward around the sides of the cake with the hands until it is within ¼ in. of the top edge, i.e. the cake bottom. Using a straight-sided jar or thick tumbler, roll firmly around the sides, pressing slightly with the other hand on the upturned bottom of the cake and turning the cake around on the sugared board when necessary. Continue rolling and turning until the sides are straight and smoothly covered and the top edges of the cake are sharp and smooth, when the process is completed and the cake is turned upright.

Allow a few days for the Almond Paste to dry before putting on the Royal Icing, or the oil from the Almond Paste will discolor it. Cover with a clean cloth to protect from dust while drying.

BOILED WHITE ICING

1 cup sugar	1 egg white,
4 tbs. water	beaten with
	flavoring

Put the sugar and water into a pan. Dissolve the sugar slowly in the water, then bring to boiling point. Boil to 240° without stirring. Brush down the sides of the pan with a brush dipped in cold water, and remove scum as it rises. Pour onto the beaten egg white and flavoring, beating constantly. Continue beating until the icing begins to thicken and coats the back of a spoon thickly. Pour quickly over the cake. Spread with a spatula, and work up the icing in swirls. You can also use the icing as a filling. The most usual additions are ½ tsp. vanilla extract or lemon juice and a pinch of cream of tartar. For other flavorings, see Butter Icings.

APRICOT GLAZE

2 tbs. apricot jam	1 tbs. water

Sieve the jam and water into a saucepan. Place over heat and bring to boiling point. Remove and cool. Use to glaze the tops of small cakes, to stick Almond Paste to Christmas cakes, etc.

BUTTER ICING OR BUTTER CREAM FILLING (1) (Quick)

4 tbs. butter *or*	Flavoring
margarine	Pinch of salt
¾ cup	Coloring
confectioners' sugar	

Cream the butter or margarine. Add the sugar and salt gradually and cream together. Beat until smooth, creamy, and pale. Add flavoring and coloring to taste.

FLAVORINGS

Almond Beat in ¼ tsp. almond extract.

Chocolate Dissolve 1 oz. chocolate in 1 tbs.

water and beat in, *or* beat in 2 tsp. cocoa and a few drops vanilla extract.

Coffee Beat in 2 tsp. strong coffee.

Jam Add 1 tbs. strong-flavored jam, e.g. plum, raspberry.

Lemon Beat in 1 tsp. strained lemon juice.

Orange Beat in 2 tsp. strained orange juice.

Vanilla Beat in ½ tsp. vanilla extract.

Walnut Add ⅜ cup chopped walnuts and 1-2 tsp. strong coffee.

In cold weather you may warm the butter slightly but do not let it oil. This butter icing always has a slight taste of raw sugar. A better but more costly one is made thus:

BUTTER ICING OR BUTTER CREAM FILLING (2)

½-¾ cup sugar	½ cup unsalted
4 egg yolks	butter (for filling)
⅝ cup milk	*or* 1 cup unsalted
	butter (for icing)
	Flavoring as
	above

Beat the egg yolks until fluffy, then gradually beat in sugar until the mixture is thick and very pale. Heat the milk and, when at boiling point, trickle it into the egg yolk mixture, beating all the time. Return the mixture to the milk saucepan and heat it gently until it thickens. Place the saucepan in a pan of cold water to cool, cover, and beat often enough to prevent a skin forming. When the custard is tepid, beat in the flavoring and butter alternately. Chill if required very stiff.

TO COLOR BUTTER ICING

Use a few drops of food coloring. These are very concentrated, so it is wise to add less than you think you need at first. Wear a rubber glove to handle the coloring, if possible, as it stains the skin. Put a tsp. white icing aside; then pour a drop or two of coloring into the lid of its bottle. Do not try to shake drops from the bottle directly into the icing. Drip the coloring into the icing from the lid. Mix the coloring in thoroughly. Test the color you have ob-

tained by holding the test tsp. of white icing beside it.

CHOCOLATE GLAZE

2 oz. plain	1-4 tbs. unsalted
chocolate	butter
1 tbs. water,	
coffee, *or* rum	

Stir the chocolate and liquid in a bowl set over a pan of very hot water until the chocolate dissolves. Remove from the heat and beat in the butter a tbs. at a time. Stand the bowl on ice or in a pan of cold water until cooled. Beat again. When it reaches the consistency you want, spread or drizzle the glaze on your cake.

CONFECTIONERS' CUSTARD

1¼ cups milk	2 tbs. sugar
3 tbs. cornstarch	½ tsp. vanilla
2 yolks *or* 1	extract
whole egg	

Blend the cornstarch with the milk, stir in the egg yolks and sugar, and cook over a gentle heat until thick. Beat in the vanilla. Allow to cool.

FONDANT OR TRANSPARENT ICING

2 cups	1¼ tsp. glucose
granulated sugar	*or* good pinch of
⅝ cup water	cream of tartar

Dissolve the sugar in the water over a low heat, add the glucose or cream of tartar, bring to a boil quickly, and boil to a temperature of 237°. Pour onto an oiled or dampened slab, let it cool slightly (if worked when too hot it will grain), and work well with a spatula, keeping the mass together as much as possible. When the paste is sufficiently cool, knead well with the hands. Wrap in paper and store in an airtight container.

When required, put into a bowl over a saucepan containing sufficient hot water to come halfway up the sides of the bowl. Stir over a very low heat until icing has the consistency of thick cream. Flavor and color as required. Allow to cool slightly before using.

FLAVORINGS

Chocolate Add 6 tsp. grated chocolate, *or* 4 tsp. cocoa, or to taste.

Coffee Stir in 4 tsp. strong coffee to taste.

GLACÉ ICING

Glacé or water icing (soft icing) is made from sifted confectioners' sugar moistened with warm water to make a thin coating consistency. It is used for icing sponges, sandwich, and layer cakes, small cakes, biscuits, and petits fours.

BASIC RECIPE

1 cup confectioners' sugar	1 tbs. warm water Flavoring Coloring

If the sugar is lumpy, break up the lumps by rolling the sugar with a rolling pin before sifting. Sift the confectioners' sugar and put into a small bowl over hot water. Add the 1 tbs. warm water gradually. Stir until all sugar is dissolved and the icing is smooth and warm. Do not allow to get too hot or the icing will lose its gloss. Add the flavoring and the coloring a drop at a time until the required shade is obtained. The icing should be thick enough to coat the back of the spoon; if too thin, add more sugar; if too thick, add more water. When of the correct consistency, cool slightly, then use at once. This quantity will coat the top of a 6-8-in. cake

Coffee Icing Add ½ tbs. strong coffee to the basic recipe, omitting ½ tbs. of the water.

Lemon Icing Substitute strained lemon juice for all or part of the water in the basic recipe. Add a few drops of coloring.

Orange Icing Substitute strained orange juice for all or part of the water in the basic recipe. Add a few drops of coloring.

CHOCOLATE GLACÉ ICING

3 oz. chocolate ¼ cup water	2 cups confectioners' sugar

Break the chocolate (preferably couverture or plain unflavored chocolate) into small pieces, put into a small bowl over a bowl of warm water, and allow to dissolve. Add the sifted confectioners' sugar and water; stir until well mixed and smooth. Use as required.

TO APPLY GLACÉ ICING

Place cakes on a wire cooling rack over a large flat dish or clean tabletop. Petits Fours and other small cakes that must be coated all over are best dipped into the icing on a fork or skewer, then drained. For large cakes the top should be fairly level. Brush off any loose crumbs. When the icing is the desired consistency, pour quickly into the center of the cake and allow to run down the sides. Avoid using a knife, if possible, but if this is necessary use a spatula dipped in hot water and dried.

If only the top is to be iced, a smooth, flat surface can be obtained easily by pinning a double thickness of waxed paper around the sides of the cake so that the paper stands 1 in. higher than the cake. Pour on the icing, which will find its own level, and allow to set. When the icing has set, remove the paper, using a knife dipped in hot water.

Put any ready-made decorations on the icing while it is still soft, but piped icing should be added after the surface is dry and firm.

GLAZES

To glaze is to make shiny. Pastry can be glazed with egg, sometimes called egg wash. Apricot or red currant glaze is used to brush over fruit tartlets, etc. Icings can be shiny too. Icings such as Chocolate Glaze are used on cakes.

GLAZES FOR PASTRY

1) Egg-wash or egg-white glaze. Brush pastry with well-beaten egg or slightly beaten egg white before baking. For a deeper color, use only the yolk, or the yolk and a little milk.
2) Sugar glazes. Fruit tarts, flans, puffs, etc., can be brushed lightly with cold

water and dredged with sugar just before baking. Sugar syrup can also be used. For a thin coat of icing, brush with beaten egg white and dredge with sugar when nearly baked, or use thin glacé icing after baking. Buns and plain cakes also can be glazed with egg white and fine or coarsely crushed sugar.

ROYAL ICING

1 lb. confectioners' sugar (approx.) 2 egg whites	1 tsp. lemon juice

If the sugar is lumpy, roll with a rolling pin before sifting. Put the egg whites into a bowl; beat slightly with a wooden spoon. Add 2 tbs. sifted sugar and beat again. Gradually add the rest of the sugar, beating well until a thick, smooth consistency and a good white color are obtained. Add the lemon juice and beat again.

If a softer icing is required, 1 tsp. glycerine may be stirred in after the sugar; this prevents brittle icing and facilitates cutting.

If the icing is not wanted at once, cover the bowl with a damp cloth to keep it soft.

TO ICE A GÂTEAU WITH ROYAL ICING

These quantities are sufficient to coat a cake of 8 in. diameter.

Place the cake, already covered with Almond Paste, on a cake board or inverted plate. Place the cake board on a turntable if available.

AMOUNTS REQUIRED

First coating Royal Icing, using 5 cups confectioners' sugar, etc., mixed to a stiff consistency.

Second coating 3-4 cups confectioners' sugar, etc., consistency to coat the back of a spoon.

Decorative piping 2 cups confectioners' sugar, etc., mixed to a stiff consistency, i.e. that will stand up in points when the back of the spoon is drawn away from the side of the bowl.

TO APPLY FIRST COATING

With a tbs. take enough icing to cover the top, and place it in the center of the cake. Spread evenly over top, smoothing the surface with a hot, wet spatula (shake or dry the spatula after dipping it in hot water as too much water softens the icing). Take up small portions of the icing with the end of the spatula, spread it smoothly around the side until the cake is completely covered and the surface smooth.

Allow to set for a few days before applying the second coat. While the icing is drying and as soon as it is hard enough, place a thin sheet of paper lightly over the top to protect it from dust.

TO APPLY SECOND COATING

Mix icing to a thin coating consistency and pour over the cake. Prick any bubbles with a fine skewer or pin; allow to firm before decorating.

TO DECORATE THE GÂTEAU WITH PIPED ICING

Cut pieces of waxed paper the same sizes as the top and sides of the cake. Sketch on these the patterns to be used for the decoration. Pin papers firmly in position on cake and prick pattern through. Mix icing to a stiff consistency and pipe design onto cake, starting at center and working outward, and finishing with the sides and base.

Using a pastry bag Decorative icing can be piped from a pastry bag and pipe. Plastic pastry bags are available. Fill the bags ⅔ full with icing and fold over the top edges. Holding the pipe between the first and second fingers force the icing through the pipe by exerting pressure with the thumbs on the top of the bag.

Icing syringes are made of metal or plastic and can be bought in sets, complete with decorative pipes. Excellent plastic turntables are also available. If colored icings are being used, the syringe must be washed before filling with another color.

All pipes must be kept clean. Always keep the bowl containing the icing covered with a damp cloth while decorating.

Petits Fours, Candies and Cookies

Petits fours and sweets called friandises are served with coffee at the end of a formal dinner and in some restaurants. Small crisp cookies are often served with a creamy dessert or ice cream, and a few rich ones, like brandy snaps, are desserts in their own right. But of course all these and other small, sweet "fancies" are eaten with afternoon tea and as café and between-meal snacks, too.

PETITS FOURS (1)

2 egg whites	A few drops
¾ cup ground	almond extract
almonds	Rice paper
¼ cup sugar	

Decoration:

Glacé cherries	Angelica

Beat egg whites very stiffly and fold in mixed almonds and sugar very lightly, with the almond extract. Place the mixture in a pastry bag fitted with a large rose vegetable pipe and force it onto rice paper in rosettes or oblongs. Decorate with small pieces of cherry and angelica and bake in a moderate to warm oven (180 °C, 350 °F) until golden brown.

20-30 Petits Fours
Cooking time – 20-30 min.

PETITS FOURS (2)

Genoese Pastry	Butter icing and
Apricot	cake crumbs
marmalade *or*	Almond paste
glaze	Glacé icing *or*
	royal icing

Cut neat shapes of Genoese Pastry squares, rings, triangles, etc. Using apricot marmalade, fasten a small piece of Almond Paste *or* some butter icing mixed with cake crumbs and flavored with vanilla, kirsch, rum, etc. neatly on top of each piece of Genoese. Coat with Glacé or Royal Icing and decorate with fine piping, scrolls, etc.

POINTS TO NOTE WHEN MAKING CANDY

1) Choose a strong thick saucepan, as any sugar mixture is liable to burn in a thin pan

109

at high temperatures. The pan should be scrupulously clean and burnished to prevent the sugar sticking.

2) Always allow the sugar to dissolve thoroughly before the mixture reaches boiling point. Tapping the bottom of the pan with a wooden spoon speeds this process. When no grittiness is felt, the sugar has dissolved completely.

3) While boiling to the required temperature, do not stir unless the recipe requires it, as stirring lowers the temperature and may make the finished sweets cloudy.

BUTTERED ALMONDS, WALNUTS, or BRAZILS

1 cup brown sugar	4 tbs. butter
6 tbs. water	3/8 cup blanched browned
2 tsp. glucose	almonds *or* dried
Pinch of cream of tartar	halved walnuts *or* whole brazils

Dissolve the sugar very slowly in the water. Add the glucose, cream of tartar, and butter. Boil to 290 °F. Have candy rings oiled and place them on an oiled slab. Place a nut in each and pour over 1/8-1/4 in. of toffee. Remove from the rings when cool and wrap separately in waxed paper and store in an airtight jar or tin.

The sweets may be made without the candy rings, if these are not available, using the toffee a little cooler and putting a teaspoonful over each nut on an oiled slab, although the finished candies will be irregular in shape.

CHOCOLATE ALMONDS

Chocolate	Almonds,
Vanilla extract	blanched and dried

Dissolve the chocolate in the smallest possible quantity of hot water and flavor it to taste with vanilla extract. Dip each almond separately and place them on an oiled slab or plates to set.

CHOCOLATE PRALINES

3/4 cup almonds	Chocolate
2 cups confectioners' sugar	Chocolate coating

Blanch the almonds and bake until brown. Chop them coarsely, then pound them finely. Place the sugar in a sugar boiler or pan, *without water*, cook until lightly browned, stir in the almonds, then pour onto an oiled slab. When cold, pound to a powder, mix with it sufficient chocolate dissolved in warm water to form a paste, and turn it into a dish. When cold, cut into squares and coat with dissolved chocolate.

COCONUT ICE

6 cups sugar	Vanilla extract
1 1/4 cups water	Red food
1/2 lb. coconut	coloring

Line a shallow pan with waxed paper. Boil the sugar and water to the "small-ball" stage (237 °F), remove the pan from the heat, add the coconut, and flavor to taste. Let it cool a little, then pour 1/2 into the prepared pan, and stand the pan containing the remainder in hot water, to prevent it setting. As soon as the portion in the pan is set, add a few drops of red food coloring to the remainder in the pan, and pour it over the ice in the pan. When cold, turn out and cut into bars.

DATES

Dates may be served plain or stuffed. To stuff: slit the date and remove the stone. Fill the cavity with a whole blanched almond or roll of Marzipan. Roll in sugar.

FONDANT

4 cups granulated sugar	2 tsp. glucose
	Colorings
1 cup water	Flavorings

Dissolve the sugar in the water, add the glucose, bring to a boil quickly, and boil until the syrup registers 237 °F ("small ball"). Pour onto an oiled or wet slab, let it cool slightly (if worked when hot it will grain), and work it with a spatula, keeping the mass together as much as possible. When the paste is sufficiently cool, knead it well with the hands. When perfectly smooth, divide into 2-3 portions, color, flavor, and knead again separately; use as required.

CRYSTALLIZED FONDANTS

6 cups sugar	Fondants
2½ cups cold water	

Dissolve the sugar in the water, then boil to the "small-thread" stage (215 °F). Pour the syrup into a bowl, cover with a damp cloth, and let it remain until perfectly cold. Place the prepared fondants on a crystallizing tray or drainer, pour the syrup over, cover with a damp cloth, and let it stand in a rather warm, dry place 9-10 hr. Drain off the syrup; let the fondants dry; pack in airtight cans.

FONDANT FRUITS or NUTS

4 cups sugar	Flavoring to
1 cup water	taste
2 tsp. glucose	Fruit *or* nuts
Coloring	

Dissolve the sugar in the water, bring to boiling point, add the glucose, and boil to the "small-ball" stage (115 °C, 237 °F). Turn onto a marble slab, work well with a spatula until white, then knead with the hands until perfectly smooth. Color and flavor to taste, put a small portion into a cup, stand the cup in a pan of boiling water, and stir until the fondant has the appearance of thick cream. Any of fruit or nuts may be dipped 1 by 1 into the liquid fondant. Coat them thoroughly; cherries, grapes, etc. may be held by the stem, but nuts must be immersed and lifted out with a ring fork. During the process, the fondant must be kept warm to prevent hardening.

FUDGE

2 cups	4 tbs. butter
granulated	½ tsp. vanilla
sugar	extract
⅝ cup milk	

Put sugar and milk in a saucepan and let soak for 1 hr. Add the butter, place over gentle heat, and stir until sugar is dissolved. Bring to boil and boil to the "small-ball" stage (237°F). Remove from heat, stir in vanilla, cool slightly, then beat until thick. Pour into an oiled pan; cut in squares when cold.

Note: Coconut, nuts, or ginger may be stirred in while fudge is cooling. **Chocolate Fudge:** Add 2 tbs. cocoa or 2 oz. plain chocolate with the butter.

HARD GLAZED FRUITS

Fresh *or* candied	¼ cup water
fruit	A few drops of
1 cup sugar	lemon juice

Fresh fruit must be dried thoroughly; candied fruit must be washed free from sugar and then dried. Dissolve the sugar in the water, add a few drops of lemon juice, and boil to the "small-crack" stage (290 °F). Plunge the saucepan into cold water to prevent the syrup becoming over-cooked, and immediately dip in the prepared fruit 1 by 1. Place them on an oiled pan until cold, then transfer to sheets of white paper.

MARSHMALLOWS

¼ lb. gum arabic	3 egg whites
1¼ cups water	Caramel flavoring
2 cups	
confectioners'	
sugar	

Soak the gum arabic in the water until soft, then heat gently until dissolved, and strain it through fine muslin. Return to the pan, add the sugar, and, when dissolved, stir in the egg whites and beat until the mixture is quite stiff. Flavor to taste, and let it remain for about 10 hr. When ready, cut into small squares and dredge them thickly with confectioners' sugar.

NOUGAT

¾ cup almonds	⅓ cup honey
2 cups	2 egg whites
confectioners'	
sugar	

Luscious sweets

Blanch and dry the almonds thoroughly. Line a box of suitable size first with white paper and then with wafer paper, both of which must be cut to fit exactly. Put the sugar, honey, and egg whites into a sugar boiler or pan, and stir over a low heat until the mixture becomes thick and white. Drop a little into cold water; if it hardens immediately remove the pan from the heat, and stir in the almonds. Dredge the slab with confectioners' sugar, turn onto it the nougat, and form into a ball. Press into the prepared box, cover with paper, let it remain under pressure until cold, then cut into squares.

PEPPERMINT CREAMS

4 cups confectioners' sugar	1-2 drops of peppermint *or* 2 tsp. peppermint extract
White of 2 large eggs	

Sift the confectioners' sugar and add the stiffly beaten egg whites and the peppermint flavoring. A very little green color may be added if liked. Mix all together well to a firm dough-like ball and roll out, well sifted with confectioners' sugar, to about $1/4$-$1/8$ in. thick. Cut out with a small round sweet cutter and leave on a wire tray to dry out for 12 hr. Pack into an airtight container. The creams may be coated with melted chocolate, if desired. For this, dissolve some broken chocolate in a bowl over hot water, holding them on a fine skewer or a sweet-dipping fork. Allow to set on clean waxed paper.

TURKISH DELIGHT

3 tbs. gelatin	$5/8$ cup water
$3/8$ cup almonds *or* $1/2$ cup pistachios	1 tbs. rum
	2 cups confectioners' sugar
1 orange	
1 lemon	1-2 tsp. cornstarch
2 cups sugar	

Put the gelatin to soak in cold water. Blanch the almonds or pistachios and chop them coarsely. Remove the rinds of the orange and lemon in thin fine strips;

place the rinds in a sugar boiler or saucepan with the sugar, $5/8$ cup water, and the strained juice of the orange and lemon. When boiling, add the gelatin, simmer until dissolved, then strain into a bowl and add the rum. Let the mixture remain until on the point of setting, then stir in the almonds or pistachios and pour at once into a moist pan. When perfectly set, turn out the gelatin, cut it into 1-in. sq. pieces, and dust them lightly in a mixture of confectioners' sugar and cornstarch.

MARZIPAN FRUIT, e.g. APPLES

Marzipan (see below) Food coloring: green, brown, red, and yellow	Angelica, cloves, etc.

Divide the Marzipan into portions, and color each portion differently. Use green marzipan to make rounded "apples," and brush lightly with red coloring; use a whole clove for a stalk, and cut "leaves" from a strip of angelica or split pistachio nuts. Make other fruit in a similar way.

For the marzipan use:

2 cups sugar	2 egg whites
1 cup water	$3/4$ cup sifted confectioners' sugar
$2 1/4$ cups ground almonds	Flavoring

Boil the sugar and water to 240 °F, then draw the sugar boiler or pan aside; when the syrup has cooled slightly, add the almonds and egg whites. Stir over a low heat for a few min., then turn onto a slab, stir in the confectioners' sugar, and work with a spatula until cool enough to handle. Knead with the hands until perfectly smooth, add flavoring, and mold into shapes.

BRANDY SNAPS

5 tbs. sugar	$1/4$ cup flour
2 tbs. butter *or* margarine	1 tsp. ground ginger
2 tbs. light corn syrup	

Cream sugar, fat, and syrup, and stir in the sifted flour and ginger. Make into 12-16 small balls and place well apart on greased baking sheets. These biscuits spread. Bake in a cool oven (150 °C, 310 °F) until a rich brown color. Allow to cool slightly; remove from sheet with a knife and, while soft enough, roll around the oiled handle of a wooden spoon; remove when set. The snaps can be filled with sweetened and flavored cream just before serving.

12-16 Brandy Snaps
Cooking time – 10-15 min.

MACAROONS (For Trifles, etc.)

2 egg whites	**½ tsp. vanilla**
½ cup sugar	**extract**
⅝ cup ground	**Rice paper** *or*
almonds	**waxed paper**
1 tsp. rice flour	**Whole blanched**
	almonds for top

Beat the egg whites stiffly in a large bowl. Mix the sugar, almonds, and rice flour together and fold into the beaten whites; add the vanilla extract. Place the rice paper or waxed paper on a baking sheet. Put the mixture into a large bag with a ½-1-in. plain pipe and pipe onto the paper in rounds about 1½ in. diameter. Place an almond in the center of each round and bake in a moderate oven (180 °C, 350 °F).

20 Macaroons Cooking time – 20-30 min.

RATAFIA BISCUITS
(For Petits Fours, Trifles, etc.)

1½ egg whites	**¾ cup ground**
2 tbs. butter	**almonds**
¾ cup sugar	**Rice paper** *or*
	waxed paper

Beat the egg whites stiffly in a large bowl. Cream the butter and sugar. Add the ground almonds and mix together well. Fold into the egg whites and mix to a smooth paste. When the mixture begins to get stiff, put it into a large bag with a plain pipe. Place the rice paper or waxed paper on a baking sheet and pipe small drops about 2 in. apart. Bake in a moderate oven (180 °C, 350 °F).

24-30 Ratafias Cooking time – about 15 min.

SPONGE FINGERS (For Charlottes, as Ice Cream Accompaniments, etc.)

⅜ cup	**Pinch of salt**
granulated	**1 tbs. sugar**
sugar	**½ cup sifted**
3 egg yolks	**flour**
1 tsp. vanilla	**¾-1 cup**
extract	**confectioners'**
3 egg whites	**sugar**

Cream the sugar and egg yolks together by beating, and beat until very light, thick and pale. Add the vanilla extract and beat well until blended.

In a separate bowl beat the egg whites and salt until fairly stiff. Sprinkle the sugar on the surface and beat again until the mixture stands in stiff peaks. Carefully spoon about ¼ of the egg white on top of the egg yolk-sugar mixture, followed by about ¼ of the sifted flour. Fold in as lightly as possible. Repeat the process 3 times, until all the mixture is added. Do not try to blend too thoroughly. It is better to leave the mixture puffy even if not fully mixed than to deflate it by stirring.

Scoop the mixture into a pastry bag and pipe onto buttered and floured baking sheets in strips 4 in. long and 1½ in. wide. Sprinkle well with confectioners' sugar. Blow to dislodge excess sugar, or invert the baking sheet and tap lightly. (The Sponge Fingers should not move.)

Bake at 150 °C, 300 °F, for about 20 min. or until the fingers are pale brown beneath and crusted outside on top. If under baked, they will be soggy when cool, so it is better to risk over-baking them slightly and making them dry.

Remove the fingers from the baking sheets with a metal spatula. Allow to cool on racks. Use them with fruit desserts of all kinds, especially charlottes and gâteaux, or serve with ice creams, bavorois, and creamy fools or custards.

24-30 Sponge Fingers

Preserves

Jams and jellies, fruit-bottling, and freezing would fill a book on their own, but some of the delicious whole-fruit preserves, especially fruits preserved in wine, brandy, or syrup, can be used with ice cream to make fancy sundaes or can be served as desserts by themselves. In the Middle East it used to be the custom to serve small portions of them to guests on arrival as a welcoming gesture; today they make an excellent "extra" to serve to guests with a sweet tooth, if you are offering a cheese selection instead of a dessert at lunch or dinner.

LEMON OR ORANGE CURD
FOR LEMON CURD USE:

3 eggs	Rind and juice
6 tbs. butter	of 2 lemons
1 cup sugar	

FOR ORANGE CURD USE:

4 eggs	Rind and juice
4 tbs. butter	of 2 oranges
1 cup sugar	and 1 lemon

Beat the eggs and put into a bowl with the butter, sugar, finely grated lemon (*or* orange) rind, and the strained juice. Place the bowl over a pan of boiling water, stir until the mixture is thick and smooth. Pour into clean warmed jars, and cover.

PEARS AND CHERRIES IN WHITE PORT

2½ cups white port *or* white wine	3 cups cherries
	16 medium pears, peeled, cored, and halved
4 cups sugar	
2½ cups water	A little yellow *or* orange coloring
Piece of cinnamon stick	

Bring the port, sugar, water, and cinnamon stick to a boil. Add the cherries (unstoned) and simmer until the syrup is thick and the cherries almost tender. Add the pear halves and bring the syrup to a boil again. Simmer 2-3 min., but do not allow the pears to soften. Pour im-

115

mediately into sterilized jars, until syrup is about to overflow, and seal.

PEACHES PRESERVED IN BRANDY

Peaches	Water
Sugar	Brandy

Dip peaches in hot water, 1 at a time, and rub off the "fur" with clean towel. Weigh. For each 1 lb. fruit allow 1½ cups sugar and 1 cup (in a measuring jug) water. Boil the sugar and water together for 10 min. without stirring. Add the peaches to the syrup and cook (only a few at a time to prevent bruising) for about 5 min., until tender. Remove the peaches from the syrup with a strainer and pack firmly into hot sterilized jars. Continue cooking the syrup, after removing peaches, until thick. Cool and measure. Add equal quantity of brandy. Bring to boiling point and fill jar of peaches to overflowing. Seal.

SEEDLESS GRAPES IN RED WINE

Prepare like Pears and Cherries in White Port, but use a fairly dry red wine instead of port, and use well-washed seedless grapes as the fruit.

Fruit bottled in brandy

Index

117